RAND AUSTRALIA and
NATIONAL SECURITY RESEARCH DIVISION

Organising for Peace Operations

Lessons Learned from Bougainville,
East Timor, and the Solomon Islands

John Gordon IV, Jason H. Campbell

T0302948

For more information on this publication, visit www.rand.org/t/RR1556

Library of Congress Cataloging-in-Publication Data is available for this publication.
ISBN: 978-0-8330-9495-7

Published by the RAND Corporation, Santa Monica, Calif.
© Copyright 2016 RAND Corporation
RAND® is a registered trademark.

Limited Print and Electronic Distribution Rights

This document and trademark(s) contained herein are protected by law. This representation of RAND intellectual property is provided for noncommercial use only. Unauthorized posting of this publication online is prohibited. Permission is given to duplicate this document for personal use only, as long as it is unaltered and complete. Permission is required from RAND to reproduce, or reuse in another form, any of its research documents for commercial use. For information on reprint and linking permissions, please visit www.rand.org/pubs/permissions.

The RAND Corporation is a research organization that develops solutions to public policy challenges to help make communities throughout the world safer and more secure, healthier and more prosperous. RAND is nonprofit, nonpartisan, and committed to the public interest.

RAND's publications do not necessarily reflect the opinions of its research clients and sponsors.

Support RAND
Make a tax-deductible charitable contribution at
www.rand.org/giving/contribute

www.rand.org

Preface

This report is for the Australian Civil-Military Centre (ACMC) in Canberra. ACMC's mission is to support the development of national civil-military capabilities to prevent, prepare for, and respond more effectively to conflicts and disasters outside Australia. ACMC sponsors research of past Australian interventions in order to determine and record important lessons that could be of value to future operations. Because of ACMC's whole-of-government perspective, the results of this research are valuable to a wide variety of agencies. As part of this report, the RAND Corporation examined the governmental organisational structures that were used in three Australian-led interventions that commenced in the late 1990s and early 2000 in the Southwest Pacific regions: **Bougainville**, **East Timor**, and the **Solomon Islands**. Interagency efforts requiring participation of many parts of the Australian Government characterised each of these operations. Importantly, each of these operations was unique, and different organisational approaches were used to manage the participation of various agencies. Numerous lessons were learned as branches of the Australian Government gained experience over time about how to interact with one another and manage complex operations such as these. The June 2015 project proposal tendered by the Australian Government is titled "Australian-led Responses to Conflict Intervention: Organisational Structures for Effective Whole-of-Government Co-ordination and Decision-Making." This research responds to Australian Government contract Activity Ref Number BP15CONC35.

The research for this report relied heavily on in-person interviews held by the authors in August 20–21 and 24–28, 2015. Although these discussions were not for attribution, a number of current and former senior Australian officials agreed to have their names listed among the participants (see Acknowledgements). While this is not an exhaustive catalogue of interviewees, in the interest of protecting participants' identities the specific dates of interviews are not provided in the citations.

This research was conducted within the International Security and Defense Policy Center of the RAND National Security Research Division (NSRD). NSRD conducts research and analysis on defence and national security topics for the U.S. and allied defence, foreign policy, homeland security, and intelligence communities and foundations and other non-governmental organisations that support defence and national security analysis.

For more information on the International Security and Defense Policy Center, see www.rand.org/nsrd/ndri/centers/isdp or contact the director (contact information is provided on web page).

Questions and comments regarding this research are welcome and should be directed to John Gordon (+ 1 (703) 413-1100, ext. 5269, email john_gordon@rand.org) or Jason Campbell (+1 (703) 413-1100, ext. 5355, email campbell@rand.org).

Contents

Figures

Summary

The Australian Civil-Military Centre (ACMC) asked the RAND Corporation to identify the organisational structures that were developed for each of the three operations in Bougainville, East Timor, and the Solomon Islands, and then analyse the environmental factors and other key considerations that impacted mission design. During the course of the research, it became apparent that, over time, numerous lessons were learned as branches of the Australian Government gained experience in how to interact with one another and manage complex operations of this type. The main body of the report describes the key Australian agencies that participated in the three operations and the roles they played. In addition to providing insights that should be useful for the preparation and conduct of operations outside Australia, the information in this report should be useful in terms of executing better whole-of-government operations inside Australian territory.

Background

From the early 20th century to the early 1970s, Australia frequently participated in military operations beyond the country's borders. Importantly, during this period, Australian military forces serving outside the country were always operating as part of a multinational coalition, normally led by the United Kingdom or the United States. Prior to the early 1970s, Australia's strategic approach could be described as forward defence, conducted as part of a coalition.

At the end of the Vietnam War, Australian defence policy under went a major change. As early as 1972, the last year of Australian participation in Vietnam, the coalition government led by Liberal Party Prime Minister William McMahon announced that the country's defence policy had to change, with greater emphasis placed on self-reliance (meaning less reliance on the United Kingdom and, especially, the United States). In 1976, the coalition government led by Prime Minister Malcolm Fraser published the country's first defence white paper, *Australian Defence*. That seminal document ushered in a new policy in which Australia's military would focus on the defence of the nation, as well as limited operations in the country's immediate vicinity. This was the so-called Defence of Australia era that lasted until the mid-1990s.

In the late 1990s, a variety of factors combined that resulted in Australia taking a leading role in multinational interventions in its region. Just prior to this period, which is the focus of this report, Australia participated in a few operations further abroad. For example, in late 1991, several hundred Australian troops were deployed as part of United Nations Transitional Authority in Cambodia (UNTAC) operation. Also in 1991, Australia contributed a small naval contingent to the Gulf War. In 1993, roughly 1100 Australian Defence Force (ADF) personnel deployed to Somalia in support of the American-led Unified Task Force operation in Somalia. Additionally, in 1994, Australia deployed more than 300 military personnel as part of the second phase of the United Nations Assistance Mission in Rwanda, which endured for two six-month contingents.

In March 1996, the Liberal-National Coalition government, led by Prime Minister John Howard, assumed power. Early in his tenure, Prime Minister Howard instituted a revision to Australia's national security planning structure, which turned out to be important for the management of the interventions that are the focus of this report. Meanwhile, in the mid-1990s, instability was increasing in Australia's immediate region.

Key Organisations in Australian Whole-of-Government Operations

National Security Committee of Cabinet

After coming to power in 1996, Prime Minister Howard created a new Cabinet organisation that would play an important role in high-level crisis planning and management: the National Security Committee (NSC) of Cabinet. Interestingly, at the time of the formation of the NSC, there was no pressing immediate crisis that required such a body. Rather, it appears that Prime Minister Howard saw the NSC as a way to promote interaction among key members of the Cabinet, of whom many (and their staffs) were new to this level of government.

The original intent of the NSC was to provide a way to systematise Cabinet-level interaction and planning on national security issues. In that regard, the list of original participants in the NSC indicates the view of the Howard government about what were the most-important agencies. Originally, the NSC was envisioned as a high-level, long-term planning and decisionmaking group. From 1997 on, the NSC structure was found to be extremely useful to coordinate and plan near-term actions, in addition to its original purpose of long-range planning.

Department of Foreign Affairs and Trade

Formed in 1987 from the merging of the Department of Foreign Affairs and Department of Trade, the Department of Foreign Affairs and Trade (DFAT) played an important role in all of the interventions examined in this report. In some cases, DFAT performed the function of lead agency within the Australian Government, or it assumed that position once the threat level reached the point that the military could assume a supporting role, exemplified by the 1999 East Timor intervention.

Prior to the time frame examined in this report, DFAT had relatively little need to interact with the other agencies that were to have key roles in these interventions. Therefore, DFAT had limited experience interacting with the ADF or the Australian Federal Police (AFP). This was an important issue, since the culture, size, capabilities, and institutional perspectives of these organisations were quite different, particularly when these interventions started in the 1998–1999 period.

In terms of the Australian Government's management of the interventions described in this report, DFAT played a central role in Bougainville and, especially, the Regional Assistance Mission to Solomon Islands (RAMSI). The organisational model used for planning and management involved DFAT creating and chairing Interdepartmental Emergency Task Forces, which would bring together other organisations from throughout the government. Depending on the location of the crisis, the task forces would be formed from the appropriate DFAT regional desk office that was managing Australian affairs in that area on a regular basis. These DFAT task forces were important in terms of facilitating whole-of-government coordination, and they were also one of the mechanisms used to provide information to the NSC.

Department of Defence and the Australian Defence Force

By the mid-1990s, the Department of Defence had been operating for two decades under a force-structure concept, the Defence of Australia, that was "primarily driven by the need to be able to defend the continent unaided."[1] Other than contributions to peacekeeping operations in Cambodia, Somalia, and Rwanda in the 1990s, as well as a few Royal Australian Navy ships that participated in Operation Desert Storm in 1991, the military and, in particular, the Army, had not conducted a significant deployment outside Australia since the end of the Vietnam War. This resulted in a general lack of an expeditionary mentality in the ADF, which had been focusing on territorial defence since the mid-1970s.

As was the case with DFAT, when this period of interventions began in the late 1990s, the ADF did not have significant experience in whole-of-government planning and operations. While a few senior ADF leaders had experience interacting with DFAT, most officers did

---

[1]   Paul Dibb, "The Self-Reliant Defence of Australia: The History of an Idea," in Ron Huisken and Meredith Thatcher, eds., *History as Policy: Framing the Debate on the Future of Australia's Defence Policy*, Canberra, Australia: Australian National University Press, 2007, p. 11.

not. In terms of the AFP, there was little military-police interaction in the years prior to the Bougainville deployment in 1998.

Perhaps most importantly in terms of different organisational perspectives, the ADF generally wanted to limit the size—and especially the duration—of its deployments for peace operations. The ADF was needed initially to establish order and control the level of violence in the intervention areas. Once that was accomplished, the ADF wanted to redeploy most of its personnel as some combination of organisations (Australian, as well as foreign entities such as the United Nations [UN]) assumed a leading role.

Australian Federal Police

In early 1998, the AFP had roughly 2,790 personnel. Then, the AFP's focus was overwhelmingly on domestic police issues, with special attention being given to preventing illegal immigration and the trafficking of illegal drugs. A few AFP personnel were deployed to locations such as Cyprus and, later that year, a handful of AFP personnel were sent to Bougainville. The AFP was not yet a significant participant in overseas interventions.

The deployment to East Timor started the process of giving the AFP the experience it needed for overseas interventions. By the time of RAMSI in 2003, the police were an early, major participant in the planning of the operation. Indeed, in the case of RAMSI, the police led in providing security on the ground in the Solomon Islands, with the ADF in support. Certainly, this was a new and different role for the police. At its peak, roughly 200 AFP personnel were deployed to RAMSI in 2003–2004.

The rapidly increasing role of the AFP in overseas interventions resulted in both an increase in strength as well as new internal organisations. By June 2004, the AFP's strength was up to some 3,470 personnel. In July of that year, it absorbed the Australian Protective Service, and the new total strength was now roughly 4,800 personnel, giving the AFP a greater ability to support protracted overseas deployments compared with five years earlier. From an organisational standpoint, an important change took place in February 2004, when the International Deployment Group (IDG) was formed. This new organisation gave the

AFP a much-better capability to manage overseas operations; the IDG included some 500 personnel, in addition to some from State and Territorial police organisations.

Australian Agency for International Development

Formed in 1974, the Australian Agency for International Development (AusAID) was a separate executive agency from 2010 until October 2013, when it was reincorporated into DFAT. At the time of the interventions described in this report, AusAID was managing assistance efforts in many of the countries in the region. Compared with the other agencies listed above, AusAID was small. In 1998, the total number of employees was roughly 580, of whom about 60 were serving outside Australia. (Though it grew considerably as an executive agency, with more than 2,100 personnel by June 2012, of whom 823 employees were serving overseas.)

In addition to being smaller than the other government organisations that played important roles in overseas involvement, AusAID's perspective was quite different. Realising that many of the nations in Australia's region are poor and underdeveloped, AusAID's perspective was a long-term. By the 1998–2003 interventions, AusAID had been involved with the counties in the region for many years. The agency's approach was based on the realisation that economic, political, and social development in the countries to Australia's north would require a long-term effort, where progress would be measured over years rather than weeks or months. This was a different view compared with several other agencies, particularly the ADF, which tended to take a short-term approach to interventions.

The following is a short summary of the lessons from each of the three operations featured in this report.

Bougainville

Australia's involvement in Bougainville stemmed from a divisive separatist conflict personified by factionalisation, failed peace processes, and escalating hostility. After roughly a decade of intermittent discussions and violence between Bougainvillean rebel groups and the government of Papua New Guinea, Australia, at the behest of the combatants, led a multinational monitoring effort comprising primarily personnel from regional states and representatives from the UN.

Though conducted in small numbers and in a permissive environment, the Bougainville operations from 1997 to 2003 proved a formative event in Australia's transition to a whole-of-government approach to carrying out complex overseas interventions. In a bureaucracy that is relatively small, the Truce Monitoring Group/Peace Monitoring Group (TMG/PMG) years were an opportunity for a new generation of civil servants and military personnel to interact and coordinate in a way that would benefit future operations where the stakes were higher and the risks greater. The Bougainville operation provided useful experience for future operations, and, as one interviewee pointed out, "Three of five members of my Bougainville team ended up in more senior positions during RAMSI." Another senior civilian official pointed out that the Bougainville experience helped DFAT work in an interagency environment and in particular get to know the ADF much better.

East Timor

In May 1999, the recently appointed transitional president of Indonesia, Bacharuddin Jusuf Habibie, signed an agreement that would permit the province of East Timor to take part in a self-determination referendum. Violence erupted, however, after the August vote overwhelmingly supported independence. In the chaos, personnel from the UN mission sent to organise and administer the ballot, the UN Assistance Mission to East Timor (UNAMET), were evacuated, and under international pressure, the Indonesian government approved the establishment of a more-robust UN peace enforcement mission. The International Force for East Timor (INTERFET) was an Australian-led multinational mission that commenced in fall 1999 and paved the way for the successful transfer of authority to the UN Transitional Administration in East Timor (UNTAET), which lasted from early 2000 until mid-2002. Finally, while the UN maintained a presence in the newly named Timor-Leste following its independence, when another string of violent riots broke out in 2006, the political office was unable to quell the hostility and, once again, an Australian-led force was sent to restore order. The Australian interventions in East Timor from 1999 to 2006 are viewed as general successes, though more to the credit of competent and motivated individuals and less on institutional efficiency.

INTERFET demonstrated to Australian officials that, while an intervention led and organised by a single entity may make things simpler, it may not be the most effective or efficient. As a former senior civilian official pointed out, "Quickly into the INTERFET mission, we learned that it was very expensive to conduct ADF-only type missions." A former senior military official took the same tone, offering, "A key lesson of INTERFET and the 1994 Operation Lagoon in Bougainville was that military planners should engage other agency planners as soon as possible." Even some of INTERFET's primary actors understood this and moved to make changes that would lead to more-inclusive policy development. Current Governor-General Sir Peter Cosgrove, while serving as Chief of the Defence Force (CDF) from 2002 to 2005, had the command and control processes revamped and designed to better integrate a whole-of-government approach. The interventions in East Timor, more so than the lower-profile Bougainville operation and in conjunction with global events, ushered in a new collective attitude throughout the Australian bureaucracy as to how a whole-of-government approach to overseas operations can help strategic interests. As a former senior civilian stated, "In only four years, we went from a 20th-century mindset into a more-complex 21st-century one," arguing that East Timor led to a new era of defence spending and investment and, importantly, changed the political environment.

Solomon Islands

In July 2003, following years of civil unrest fuelled by ethnic tensions, widespread corruption, and increasing criminality, the parliament of the Solomon Islands approved a request by its prime minister,

Albert Kamakeze, for outside assistance to restore law and order and help prevent a governmental collapse. A small international monitoring force established in 2000 to oversee disarmament efforts—tied to an earlier ceasefire agreement—proved insufficient to foster sustainable peace; this new mission would be much more robust. RAMSI, like Bougainville and East Timor, was an Australian-led multinational mission. More so than its predecessors, however, RAMSI would rely on the collective efforts of military, police, and civilian personnel who would take on responsibilities for which they were uniquely qualified in a coordinated manner. Thus, while the experiences of Bougainville and East Timor would inform both policymakers and implementers, RAMSI would introduce new challenges to the whole-of-government concept.

While there are many lessons from RAMSI that should be incorporated into any future whole-of-government intervention, it must be stated clearly that, among those interviewed, the operation on the whole represented a great achievement of interagency coordination. As a former senior civilian official proclaimed, "RAMSI was the best example of a whole-of-government effort I saw in 13 years at DFAT." Another former senior civilian said that they have never experienced before or since that level of interagency coordination in the Australian bureaucracy. A former senior military official argued that, in general, there needs to be a clear concept of mission and political conviction for these types of missions to succeed. The official praised the senior levels of the Australian Government for providing this, at least at the beginning. The official went on, however, to state that the "timing drifted" and that, "Our mandate was clear, but many aspects were left openended. We were not definitive on what constituted success or the end of the mission."

The military and civilian planners of the RAMSI mission took lessons from their East Timor and Bougainville experiences. Generally, the earlier experience proved to be good guidance for RAMSI. However, more consideration could have been taken in the planning phase to acclimatise the collection of interagency partners to the capabilities and limitations of their partner agencies.

Overarching Whole-of-Government Insights

The mission, the size, and the duration of the three interventions examined in this report differed in important ways. Therefore, some of the insights and lessons are specific to a particular intervention. In other respects, there are important overarching insights that can be drawn from examining Bougainville, East Timor, and the Solomon Islands as a continuum. The next sections detail some of the most-important issues that emerged from these operations and lessons for the future.

The NSC Provided a Structure for Whole-of-Government Coordination

It may be an example of a fortunate coincidence (recall that there were no immediate foreign crises looming when the NSC was formed), but the Howard government's 1996 creation of the NSC, including its supporting processes that reached down into various Cabinet ministries, was a significant step toward facilitating a whole-of-government approach to overseas interventions.

Subsequent Australian Governments have used the NSC to varying degrees. That the NSC continues to be used today at the highest level of the Australian Government is indicative of its usefulness.

The Relatively Small Size of the Australian Government Allowed for Important Personal Relationships to Be Built That Were Key to Both Within-Agency and Whole of Government Coordination

Many interviewees stressed the point that interactions among senior personnel within and among agencies were fundamental to enabling an interagency approach. Whether it was taking place in Canberra, or on the ground in East Timor or the Solomon Islands, the ability—and willingness—to have frequent, regular interaction at the senior- and upper-middle management levels greatly aided the interagency process.

Even within agencies, the personal relationships among senior personnel meant that lessons learned (including what worked well and what were problems) from ongoing operations could be quickly disseminated among senior personnel. In some cases, those insights directly influenced successive operations. For example, Governor-

General Cosgrove's important experiences as the commanding general of INTERFET shaped some of the guidance he would later issue while serving as CDF to ADF personnel deploying to the Solomon Islands. The relatively small size of the ADF contributed directly to this process.

Interagency Processes Were Developed and Evolved over Time

Because of the nature of these interventions (including major international considerations, modest-to-low threat levels, and the need for holistic multiagency approaches to achieve national policy objectives), it was appropriate that DFAT be the lead agency in most cases. The one exception was the initial planning for INTERFET, where the ADF was clearly in the lead for the critical initial phase of the intervention. INTERFET preparations had to be accomplished quickly, and the intervention included the possibility that fighting could take place in East Timor or perhaps even with Indonesia. In those circumstances, it was appropriate that the military have the leading role, at least for the first few months. Even in that case, other agencies participated and were increasingly included as the intervention transitioned toward a more stable, long-term operation.

Below the NSC level, one of the most important processes that was created to foster whole-of-government cooperation was Interdepartmental Emergency Task Forces, typically directed by DFAT. Once the role of the task forces became clear throughout government, they became an accepted and useful means to facilitate whole-of-government actions for both planning and during the execution phase of an operation.

Agency Cultures and Processes Differed, but Understanding Improved over Time

The internal culture of DFAT is different than the ADF. The police are not the same as the military. AusAID is also different. These differences in organisational culture and perspectives should have been expected and are probably not only unavoidable, but can be considered a positive attribute, since different approaches to a problem can be useful. However, for organisations that are not familiar with one another, it can be challenging to gain an understanding of how business is done and problems are approached. In the earlier years covered in this report, the lack of familiarity with different processes and culture was the source of tension and misunderstanding.

The general lack of familiarity among the various agencies of government in the late 1990s and early 2000s is understandable and perhaps unavoidable given the bureaucratic culture of the post–Vietnam era with respect to security. There was little need or incentive for the AFP and ADF, for example, to work with each other from the mid-1970s to the late 1990s. Therefore, the culturally based interagency challenges that were apparent in Bougainville, INTERFET, and RAMSI are understandable.

As time passed, DFAT, the police, and military became more familiar with one another. Together, they learned what it was like to plan and operate together. By the time of RAMSI, the ADF was comfortable assuming a supporting role to the AFP. Although the two organisations were still learning about how to better integrate their planning and operations, this was a much-better situation compared with the circumstances of the late 1990s, when there was essentially no interaction between the police and military.

Possible Challenges of Future Operations

The following are a number of issues that were observed in every intervention that resulted in tensions within the whole-of-government process. These are issues that merit examination to see whether they have been addressed or still remain as potential challenges in the future.

Unrealistic Expectations as to How Long Interventions Will Last

In each of the three cases considered in this report, there was an expectation (or perhaps a hope) that the intervention would be relatively short and include a clear and comprehensive disengagement process. This tended to be particularly the case among ADF leadership. The Bougainville operation was initiated to address a crisis but was gradually reduced to the point that senior leadership in Canberra had to be informed that any further cuts would make continuing the mission impossible. In the case of INTERFET, it was the expectation of the Australian Government that the UN would quickly be able to assume the vast majority of the responsibility for helping post-independence East Timor. For some agencies, particularly the ADF, RAMSI was also largely built around assumptions that the intervention would be of relatively short duration. In no case was the expectation of a relatively short intervention or a smooth, deliberate transition valid.

Intelligence, Reporting, and Information-Passing Procedures of Agencies Varied

A number of interviewees highlighted that intelligence, reporting, and information sharing procedures among agencies varied. They stated that, despite the steadily improving whole-of-government processes, there remained significant differences in the way agencies managed both information and intelligence. For example, several ADF interviewees pointed out that the military closely manages the dissemination of reports and information coming out of the operational area. According to the military, when DFAT reports were generated and the information passed from the field back to Canberra, the information would quickly be disseminated throughout the entire Australian Government. While neither method is objectively improper, each reflects different perspectives on information management that, on a number of occasions, resulted in interagency tension.

Advantages Exist in the Interpersonal Relationships, but This Could Result in Vulnerabilities in the Future

There are advantages to the relatively small size of the military and international affairs system in Australia. Senior leaders could and did build relationships both within and among agencies that were based on trust. This was a regularly recurring theme that we heard from current and former personnel of every agency interviewed.

There are, however, potential disadvantages and vulnerabilities that can result from this way of doing business. Key personnel eventually move to new jobs and, of course, retire. Although retirees will still be available for some time and are potentially useful sources of information and lessons from past operations, they will not be available forever. This Australian system of relying on relationships among senior personnel clearly had advantages and probably facilitated the rapid passing of lessons within and among agencies.

Australia was successful in each of the three operations examined in this report. The good relationships that existed among the upper-middle and senior leaders who planned and conducted these missions were instrumental in making these operations successful. What appeared to be lacking was a more-systematic way of ensuring that the high-level lessons are captured within each agency that is involved, as well as fixing responsibility so that some organisation within the government can examine the whole-of-government lessons that any major operation will produce.

Significantly Different Approaches Were Used to Manage Personnel in Interventions

There were significant differences in how long agencies deployed personnel to these operations. In keeping with the general aversion of the military toward getting overly committed to this type of operation, deployment times for the military were normally three to six months, with the shorter end of the spectrum being the norm. Both DFAT and police officials seconded to the operations tended to deploy personnel longer; in some cases, over a year. Often, AusAID officials not formally tied to the operations but active in the same areas were relied upon to contribute to development efforts. Theirs was the typical two- to three-year tour served by Australian diplomats abroad.

The different approaches to deployment lengths meant that there was considerable variation in experience level of the personnel from the various agencies. DFAT representatives mentioned on several occasions that their representatives on the ground saw a constant turnover of ADF personnel, noting that the newly arrived military members would barely learn the details of what was happening in the area before it was time to rotate. It was also noted by several interviewees that, depending on the agency, the different deployment lengths affected morale of personnel on the ground. In the future, there may be advantages to taking a more-consistent approach to deployment times, while realising that the level of activity an agency is experiencing can have significant impact on its ability to manage personnel.

Another personnel-management issue was the difficulty some agencies had in getting personnel, particularly civilians, to volunteer for these operations. In the future, one of the conditions for employment in some agencies may have to include a provision that new hires accept the fact that overseas deployments may be periodically required.

Future Operations Would Benefit from Earlier and More-Inclusive Whole-of-Government Campaign Planning

There were varying amounts of time available to plan for the three operations that were the focus of this research. Even within particular operations, there were different amounts of planning time available to the various elements of the Australian Government (e.g., the RAMSI intervention, where DFAT and the AFP had considerable amounts of planning lead time, but the military's operational units were given much-shorter warning of the operation). In future operations, all agencies within the Australian Government would benefit from a uniform starting point for planning and a whole-of-government approach starting as soon as it is determined that a multiagency operation was looming. This process should include a clear delineation of roles, responsibilities, and accountabilities among agencies.

Acknowledgements

The RAND Corporation's research was made possible by the great assistance we received from many individuals in Australia and the United States. The research was sponsored by the Australian Civil-Military Centre (ACMC), whose director, Alan Ryan, was instrumental in opening many high-level doors for the research team. Also at ACMC, Judy Swann served as the primary point of contact for the research. She organised the weeklong interview schedule in August 24–28, 2015, the period when the team was in Canberra.

Prior to the research team departing for Canberra, several interviews were conducted with former Australian officials in Sydney in August 20–21, 2015. These included Annmaree O'Keeffe and Alan Dupont. We thank these individuals who generously offered their time for interviews. The majority of the interviews were conducted in Canberra. Of those, all but a few were face-to-face meetings that took place at locations throughout the city. In a few cases, interviews were conducted by phone when someone could not be in Canberra. It should be noted that an agreement was reached with ACMC and the interviewees that we would not use their names directly in the text of the report, unless the interviewee explicitly indicated to us that their name could be attributed to a particular issue or quote. For that reason, the text includes numerous references to current or former Australian officials, rather than the names of specific individuals.

Numerous persons were interviewed for our research. Not all are named below, but we want to extend special thanks to selected individuals. Current or former Australian Defence Force (ADF) members who were interviewed included the Governor-General Sir Peter Cosgrove;

Chief of Army Lieutenant General Angus Campbell; Major General John Frewen, the Head of Military Strategic Commitments; retired Major Generals Peter Abigail, Jim Molan, Roger Powell, and Michael Smith; and retired Brigadier Chris Appleton. These current or former senior officers generously made time available for discussions. In every case, their personal experiences and detailed insights were invaluable to the research process. Also from the ADF was retired Lieutenant Colonel and historian Bob Breen, who not only made himself available for an in-person meeting, but also alerted us to a number of documents that were helpful in the research.

From the Department of Foreign Affairs and Trade (DFAT), the interviewees included the Deputy Secretary Ewen McDonald, Ric Wells, Fred Smith, Rohan Titus, and Rob Tranter. The candid insights of these individuals clarified many issues related to how DFAT coordinated most of the interventions that were the subject of the research. Among the former DFAT officials who met with us were Nick Warner and James Batley; they had leading roles in the initial years of the Regional Assistance Mission to Solomon Islands intervention and provided useful insights on the other operations that were under consideration.

From the Australian Federal Police (AFP), the insights provided by Superintendent Tim Dahlstrom were of great value. His explanation of how the AFP evolved into international operations during this era put the role of the AFP in relation to the other agencies of government in clear perspective.

Peter Jennings, the executive director of the Australian Strategic Policy Institute, provided important information on how the NSC of Prime Minister John Howard was formed; the organisation was of critical importance during the course of our research. Finally, Ric Smith, a retired official who lists among his numerous former titles ambassador and Secretary of the Department of Defence, provided invaluable insights on the functioning of the Australian bureaucracy, both from a whole-of-government and departmental perspective.

At RAND, this research was conducted within Seth Jones's International Security and Defense Policy Program. Seth provided helpful guidance and direction early in the research process. Jennifer

Moroney, director of RAND Australia, provided assistance in multiple ways, including helping coordinate interviews, conducting interviews, making her office available to the research team while they were in Australia, and helping open doors with key officials in the country. Nancy Pollock of the RAND National Defense Research Institute was instrumental in assisting the team in administrative arrangements for the project.

Abbreviations

ACMC	Australian Civil-Military Centre
ADF	Australian Defence Force
AFP	Australian Federal Police
ASTJIC	Australian Theatre Joint Intelligence Centre
AUD	Australian dollar
AusAID	Australian Agency for International Development
BRA	Bougainville Revolutionary Army
CDF	Chief of the Defence Force
CIMIC	civil-military cooperation
CTF	Combined Task Force
DFAT	Department of Foreign Affairs and Trade
DIO	Defence Intelligence Organisation
ETPU	East Timor Policy Unit
GDP	gross domestic product
IDETF	Interdepartmental Emergency Task Forces
IDG	International Deployment Group
IWG	Interdepartmental Working Group

INTERFET	International Force for East Timor
IPMF	International Peace Monitoring Force
MP	Member of Parliament
NGO	nongovernmental organisation
NSC	National Security Committee
NZDF	New Zealand Defence Force
ONA	Office of National Assessments
PMG	Peace Monitoring Group
PNG	Papua New Guinea
PPF	Participating Police Force
RAMSI	Regional Assistance Mission to Solomon Islands
RAN	Royal Australian Navy
SCD	Strategic Command Division
SCNS	Secretaries Committee on National Security
SPCG	Strategic Policy Coordination Group
TMG	Truce Monitoring Group
UN	United Nations
UNAMET	United Nations Assistance Mission to East Timor
UNTAC	United Nations Transitional Authority in Cambodia
UNTAET	United Nations Transitional Administration in East Timor
VTC	video teleconferencing

CHAPTER ONE

Introduction

This report is for the Australian Civil-Military Centre (ACMC) in Canberra. ACMC's mission is to support the development of national civil-military capabilities to prevent, prepare for, and respond more effectively to conflicts and disasters outside Australia. Because of the inherently whole-of-government nature of most overseas operations, ACMC's staff includes representatives from various parts of the Australian Government, including the Australian Defence Force (ADF), the Australian Federal Police (AFP), and the Department of Foreign Affairs and Trade (DFAT).

As part of its mission, ACMC sponsors research of past Australian interventions in order to determine and record important lessons that could be valuable to future operations. Because of ACMC's whole-of-government perspective, the products of this report are of value to a wide variety of agencies.

Research Design

This RAND Corporation report examines the governmental organisational structures that were used during three Australian-led interventions in the Southwest Pacific region: **Bougainville**, **East Timor**, and the **Solomon Islands**. Each of these operations was an interagency effort that required participation of many parts of the Australian Government. Importantly, each of these operations was unique, and different organisational approaches were used to manage the participation of various agencies.

This report examines each of these operations, focusing acutely on how the government organised for each intervention and what the main lessons were. The report is not intended to provide a detailed account of how each intervention unfolded on the ground or to highlight the numerous operational and tactical level insights that were revealed. It also does not cover in great detail certain strategically imperative efforts that contributed greatly to the operations, such as coalition building. Rather, the goal of this report is to examine interagency issues and determine what went right, what the main challenges were, and what the most important insights are for the future.[1] Thus, this report is decidedly Canberra-centric in its perspective and incorporates theatre-level events only insofar as they correlate to strategic themes deliberated and decided on by the Australian bureaucracy or to provide necessary context. The research involved a mixture of techniques. There is a body of literature on the three operations, some of which was published in Australia, while other documents are from outside Australia (primarily the United States). In addition to publicly available books, research papers, and articles, Australian official sources were examined to the extent that they were available. Interestingly, we discovered that there is not a large body of unclassified official reports available on these interventions. That reality made the third element of the research—interviews—particularly important.

The research team was in Australia in August 20–30, 2015, during which numerous interviews with current and former Australian military and civilian officials took place. Some had experience that spanned all three operations, whereas others were only involved with one or two of the interventions. Importantly, it was agreed that the names of the interviewees would not be directly quoted in this report to protect their confidentiality. The Acknowledgements section of the report provides a list of names of the primary interviewees with whom we met.

---

[1] The contributing information in this chapter was derived from Australian Government reporting, open-source research, and interviews conducted by the authors during a research trip to Australia in August 2015.

Background

Before looking at each of the three operations that are the main focus of the report, it is important to review how the Australian Government was structured to conduct these missions in 1998–2006. Additionally, this section provides background information on the government agencies that led roles in these operations.

From the early 20th century to the early 1970s, Australia frequently participated in military operations beyond the country's borders. During the two World Wars, tens of thousands of Australian troops fought in the Middle East and many parts of the South Pacific (Malaya, New Guinea, the Solomon Islands, and Borneo). In the late 1940s and 1950s, Australian troops were engaged in Malaya and Korea. Some 60,000 Australians served in South Vietnam in 1962–1972. Importantly, during this period, Australian military forces serving outside the country were always operating as part of a multinational coalition, normally led by the United Kingdom or the United States. Prior to the early 1970s, Australia's strategic approach could be described as forward defence, conducted as part of a coalition.

At the end of the Vietnam War, Australian defence policy underwent a major change. As early as 1972, the last year of Australian participation in Vietnam, the coalition government led by Liberal Party Prime Minister William McMahon announced that the country's defence policy had to change, with greater emphasis placed on self-reliance (meaning less reliance on the United Kingdom and, especially, the United States). In 1976, the Australian coalition government headed by Prime Minister Malcolm Fraser published *Australian Defence*, the country's first defence white paper. This seminal document introduced a new force structure policy in which Australia's military would focus on the defence of the nation, as well as limited operations in the country's immediate vicinity.[2] Emphasis was placed on the Royal Australian Air Force and Navy to defend the northern approaches to the country,

---

[2] Hugh White, "Four Decades of the Defence of Australia: Reflections on Australian Defence Policy over the Past 40 Years," in Ron Huisken and Meredith Thatcher, eds., *History as Policy: Framing the Debate on the Future of Australia's Defence Policy*, Canberra, Australia: Australian National University Press, 2007.

with the Australian Army focusing on preventing an incursion into the country's northern regions. While small numbers of Australian military personnel and police participated in various United Nations (UN) operations in this period, it was not until 1987, when a small Australian force was deployed to Fiji in response to a coup in that nation (Operation Morris Dance), that Australian troops were used in an overseas operation. And, even in this case, the forces were ultimately not required to make a landing and were kept at sea. It should be noted that, throughout this period, the country remained engaged in its immediate region, including providing assistance to Papua New Guinea (PNG) and the Solomon Islands. Additionally, Australian policymakers at the time were concerned about events in Indonesia, as that nation endured periods of instability from the 1960s into the 1990s.

In the 1990s, a variety of factors resulted in Australia taking a leading role in multinational interventions in its region. First, in late 1991, several hundred Australian troops deployed as part of UN Transitional Authority in Cambodia (UNTAC) operation. While this was a UN-sponsored operation, UNTAC increased Australia's role in the region. Then, in 1993, Australia deployed a battalion group to Somalia in support of a United States–led peace-enforcement operation that would be transitioned to the UN. Finally, from 1994 to 1996, Australia remained active on the African continent, sending two contingents of forces to support the UN Assistance Mission in Rwanda. Australia also contributed a small naval contingent to the Gulf War in 1991.

In March 1996, the Liberal Party and National Party coalition government led by Prime Minister John Howard assumed power. Early in his tenure, Prime Minister Howard instituted a reorganisation of Australia's national security planning structure that proved important for the management of the interventions that are the focus of this report. These organisational reforms will be described in the following section. Meanwhile, in the mid-1990s, instability was increasing in Australia's immediate region.

A number of Australia's neighbours to the north and east are small, poor, and fragile states. For example, PNG became independent in 1975. In 1999–2000, PNG had a per capita gross domestic product (GDP) of roughly $3,500 Australian dollars (AUD). The nearby Solomon Islands achieved independence in 1978. Per capita GDP in 1999 was roughly similar to PNG, approximately $3,600 AUD.[3] Australia has provided assistance to both countries since they achieved independence. For example, the Australian Agency for International Development (AusAID) was heavily involved in PNG since 1975.[4] By the mid-1990s, there was increasing instability in both PNG and the Solomon Islands.

Australia's other northern neighbour, Indonesia, is much larger in terms of both size and population than PNG or the Solomon Islands. Indonesia was plagued with internal troubles and tensions long before achieving independence in 1949. In the late 1990s, Indonesia experienced considerable economic difficulty; its per capita GDP was similar to PNG and the Solomon Islands, roughly $4,000 AUD. However, pockets of Indonesia had considerably fewer resources. The per capita GDP of East Timor, one of the case studies in this report, was roughly $2,300 AUD.[5] To put these numbers in perspective, the per capita GDP in Australia in 1999–2000 was approximately $31,000 AUD.

One of the first interventions by Australia in its region in the 1990s was Operation Lagoon, which took place over three weeks in October 1994. The mission provided security for a peace conference between the PNG government and the Bougainville Revolutionary Army (BRA). Several hundred ADF personnel, primarily from the Australian Army's high-readiness 3rd Brigade, deployed to Bougainville on short notice. Because BRA elected to not participate, the actual conference was not successful. However, the operation did give the ADF some experience in both interagency and coalition planning because of

---

[3] Central Intelligence Agency, "The World Factbook: Australia-Oceania: Solomon Islands," February 29, 2016a; Central Intelligence Agency, "The World Factbook: Australia-Oceania: Papua New Guinea," March 1, 2016b.

[4] Australian Agency for International Development, *The Contribution of Australian Aid to Papua New Guinea's Development, 1975–2000*, Evaluation and Review Series No. 34, Canberra, Australia, June 2003, pp. ix–xvi.

[5] Conversion rates from U.S. to Australian dollars based on 75 U.S. cents per $1 AUS. (Central Intelligence Agency, "The World Factbook: East and Southeast Asia: Indonesia," April 18, 2016c).

the need to coordinate with New Zealand and DFAT's important role in planning the operation.[6]

In early 1997, the so-called Sandline Affair took place in PNG. This incident involved the Prime Minister of PNG contracting for mercenaries from the United Kingdom–based military services organisation Sandline International. PNG Prime Minister Julius Chan, frustrated by unsuccessful attempts to negotiate with rebels on Bougainville and unable to gain support from Australia and New Zealand to use force against the rebel groups, intended to use Sandline International to attack the rebels on the island. This effort collapsed and nearly led to a coup by the PNG military; Chan's government was brought down by the incident. The Sandline affair clearly demonstrated to the still-new Howard government in Canberra the growing level of instability in Australia's near region.[7] This incident also had the effect of bringing about negotiations between the PNG government and the rebels on Bougainville, which led directly to the first Australian-led intervention examined in this report. The decades-long Defence of Australia era was about to come to an end.

Key Organisations in Australian Whole-of-Government Operations

Before specific cases are examined, we will review the most-important organisations that Australia used in 1998–2006 to decide policy and manage the interventions that are the focus of this report. Several important factors came together in the late 1990s that resulted in the need for Australia to intervene in its immediate region. Instability in the immediate region was growing: an increasingly restive separatist movement in East Timor, strife in Bougainville, and tension in the Sol-

---

[6] Australian Peacekeeper and Peacemaker Veterans Association, "Operation Lagoon," undated.

[7] Derek Barry, "Woolly Days: The Sandline Crisis 10 Years On," Woolly Days website, February 11, 2007.

omon Islands. What organisations and structures were at Canberra's disposal in order to manage these varied crisis situations?

National Security Committee of Cabinet

Soon after coming to power in 1996, Prime Minister Howard created a new Cabinet organisation that would play an important role in high-level crisis planning and management, the National Security Committee (NSC). Interestingly, at the time of its formation, there was no pressing immediate crisis that required the creation of such a body. Rather, it appears that Prime Minister Howard saw the NSC as a way to promote interaction among key members of the Cabinet, of which many (and their staffs) were new to this level of government. The 1996 NSC included:[8]

- John Howard, Prime Minister (Chair, NSC)
- Tim Fischer, Member of Parliament (MP), Deputy Prime Minister, Minister for Trade
- Peter Costello, MP, Treasurer (Deputy Chairman)
- Alexander Downer, MP, Minister of Foreign Affairs
- Ian McLachlan, MP, Minister for Defence
- Daryl Williams, MP, Attorney General, and Minister for Justice.

The original intent of the NSC was to provide a way to systematise Cabinet-level interaction and planning on national security issues. In that regard, the list of original participants in the NSC indicates the Howard government's views about the importance of specific agencies. Originally, the NSC was envisioned as a high-level, long-term planning and decision-making group. While the NSC was formed at a time of no immediate crisis, from 1997 on the NSC structure was found to be extremely useful to coordinate and plan near-term actions, in addition to its original purpose of long-range planning.

The creation of institutional mechanisms to support the NSC was an important additional benefit. These included the Secretaries Com-

---

[8] AustralianPolitics.com, "Howard Government 1996 Cabinet Committees," March 17, 1996.

mittee on National Security (SCNS) and the Strategic Policy Coordination Group (SPCG). The SCNS consists of secretaries of departments and heads of agencies with responsibilities for national security issues. The focus of the SPCG is international security issues that affect Australia. Within the Australian Department of Defence, a Strategic Watch Group was established to monitor potential crises, and a Strategic Operations Division was created within the ADF to conduct interdepartmental liaison (see Figure 1.1). These entities performed staff and coordination functions to support the NSC members and helped coordinate the input from various agencies, such as DFAT task forces, outlined in this report.

The new NSC was tested during the 1997 Sandline Affair. Shortly thereafter, this structure was used to make high-level decisions

Figure 1.1
Australia's National Crisis Management Organisation, with Emphasis on the Department of Defence's Corresponding Structure, 1999

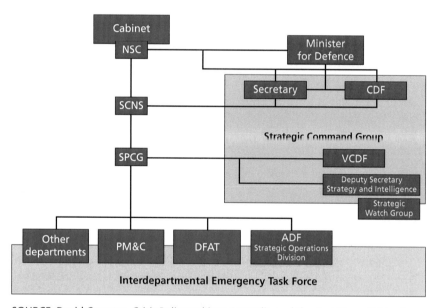

SOURCE: David Connery, *Crisis Policymaking: Australia and the East Timor Crisis of 1999, Canberra*, Australia: Australian National University Press, 2010, p. 14.
NOTE: CDF = Chief of the Defence Force; PM&C = Prime Minister and Cabinet; VCDF = Vice Chief of the Defence Force.
RAND RR1556-1.1

and review ongoing actions during the Bougainville intervention in 1998 and was found to work well. Next, the NSC dealt with the 1999 East Timor intervention, a large and potentially dangerous operation that included the possibility of violence. Again, the NSC structure proved useful for both planning and monitoring day-to-day operations in East Timor. Indeed, there were periods during the East Timor intervention where the NSC met daily.

By the time of the 2003 intervention in the Solomon Islands (Regional Assistance Mission to Solomon Islands [RAMSI]), the NSC process was well established, including the mechanisms of staff interaction by the various agencies that supported the NSC. At the NSC level, planning for RAMSI started about ten months prior to the deployment of Australian forces to the Solomon Islands.

Department of Foreign Affairs and Trade

Formed in 1987 from the merging of the Department of Foreign Affairs and Department of Trade, DFAT had an important role in the interventions examined in this report. In some cases, DFAT performed the function of lead agency within the Australian Government, or it assumed that position once the threat level reached a point that the military could assume a supporting role, as exemplified by the 1999 East Timor intervention. During most of the period examined in this report, Ashton Calvert served as the Secretary of DFAT (April 1998–January 2005). He was succeeded by Michael L'Estrange (January 2005–August 2009).

DFAT's major responsibilities involve promoting Australia's regional and global interests. Although it deals with immediate, near-term crises, DFAT also has to take a long-term perspective toward Australia's relations with its neighbours.

DFAT's relatively small size is a limiting factor. In June 1999, shortly before the International Force for East Timor (INTERFET) intervention in East Timor—an important event for Australia—the total DFAT worldwide staff was 3,633. This figure includes some 1,610 locally engaged persons in embassies and other sites outside Australia.[9] It should be noted that the personnel totals listed here do not include AusAID, since DFAT did not assume direct control of that organisation until 2013. One of the consequences of DFAT's relatively small size is that there is little excess capacity available to respond to a sudden crisis and, in the event of a protracted intervention, the need to devote personnel to that particular event for an extended period can be a strain on normal operations.

In terms of the Australian Government's management of the interventions described in this report, DFAT had a central role in Bougainville and, especially, RAMSI. The organisational model used for planning and management was for DFAT to create and chair the Interdepartmental Emergency Task Forces (IDETFs), which brought together other organisations from throughout the government. Depending on the location of the crisis, the task forces formed from the appropriate DFAT regional desk office that managed Australian affairs in that area on a regular basis. These DFAT task forces were important in terms of facilitating whole-of-government coordination, and they were also one of the mechanisms used to provide information to the NSC. The severity of the crisis determined the length a particular task force would be in existence. Eventually, a determination was made to return to the normal regional desk office mode of operations. It should be noted that the initial planning for the 1999 INTERFET intervention was overwhelmingly in the hands of the ADF, with DFAT taking a supporting role. Once the situation in East Timor stabilised, roles were reversed, and DFAT assumed its normal lead-agency function.

All of the interventions featured in this report were coalition operations, with Australia leading and managing a multinational operation. DFAT had the leading role in coordinating policy issues with other nations that participated in these interventions. While DFAT led in terms of multinational issues, the ADF always coordinated directly with its military counterparts in the various countries that participated in the operation. Indeed, the ADF also coordinated with the militaries

---

[9]   Australian Government, Australian Department of Foreign Affairs and Trade, "Appendix 3," in *Annual Report, 1999–2000*, Canberra, Australia, October 3, 2000.

of countries that were not part of the actual operation, but whose cooperation was essential, most importantly Indonesia and PNG.

Another important organisational innovation used during the RAMSI intervention was the creation of a special coordinator to manage whole-of-government operations on the ground. Significantly, DFAT provided the special coordinator, which by all accounts worked well in terms of managing interagency actions. The details of this position and how it functioned will be described in Chapter Four.

Prior to the time frame described in this report, DFAT had relatively little need to interact with other agencies that had key roles in these interventions. Therefore, DFAT had limited experience interacting with the ADF or the AFP. This was an important issue, since the culture, size, capabilities, and institutional perspectives of these organisations were quite different, particularly when these interventions started in 1998–1999. In particular, DFAT had little prior experience in dealing with the AFP. In terms of the ADF, the cultural differences were considerable. The military places considerable emphasis on detailed planning prior to and during operations. DFAT was (and still is today) limited in terms of size, a fact that influenced the number of personnel that could be devoted to planning. At times, this was frustrating to the ADF, since the military developed detailed plans for its portion of each of these missions and was often expecting more-detailed guidance from DFAT compared with what was actually provided. Interestingly, we heard this comment several times from ADF and DFAT personnel. Although there was clearly a general lack of DFAT familiarity with the ADF and AFP in 1998–1999, as whole-of-government experience was gained from 1998 to 2006, the level of understanding among these agencies improved considerably.

Department of Defence and the Australian Defence Force

By the mid-1990s, the Department of Defence had been operating for two decades under the Defence of Australia force structure concept. The early 1990s brought missions to Cambodia and Rwanda in support of UN operations and a deployment to Somalia as part of an American-led (and UN sanctioned) effort there. A few Royal Australian Navy ships also participated in Operation Desert Storm in 1991.

While important contributions to coalition missions, these operations were limited by time and/or force levels and did not compare with the Australian's last significant deployment outside Australia, Vietnam. This was indicative of a general lack of an expeditionary mentality in the ADF, which had been focusing its force structure on territorial defence since the mid-1970s. In terms of military capabilities, there were relatively few military ships and aircraft to deploy the Army and then support overseas operations. Training and readiness levels of the mid-1990s reflected the decades-long focus on territorial defence. The ADF of 1998 consisted of roughly 52,900 active-duty military personnel. Of that, 24,100 were in the Army, the service that would have the largest burden in the upcoming interventions. All branches of the military were experiencing modest difficulties in recruiting and retaining personnel in this period.[10]

As was the case with DFAT, when this period of interventions began in the late 1990s, the ADF did not have a lot of experience in whole-of-government planning and operations. While a few senior ADF leaders were experienced in interacting with DFAT, most officers were not. In terms of the AFP, there was little military-police interaction in the years prior to the Bougainville deployment in 1998.

The different perspectives toward planning in DFAT and the ADF have been discussed, but there were other important differences in perspective and culture. For example, DFAT tended to send its staff to foreign countries for a year or more and, in the case of AusAID, it was not unusual for its staff to deploy for three years or longer. Once the AFP became heavily involved in foreign interventions, its personnel tended to remain in the operational area for a year or longer. The ADF's perspective on deployments was to rotate most personnel based on three- to six-month tours of duty. From the perspective of the other agencies (DFAT and AFP), this resulted in its representatives dealing with the constant rotation of ADF leadership in the operational area.

Perhaps most importantly, in terms of different organisational perspectives, the ADF generally wanted to limit the size—and especially

---

[10] Australian Government, Department of Defence, *Defence Annual Defence Report 1998–1999*, Canberra, Australia, 1999, pp. 247–249.

the duration—of its deployments for peace operations. The ADF was needed to initially establish order and ensure the level of violence was under control in the intervention areas. Once that was accomplished, the ADF wanted to redeploy most of its personnel as some combination of organisations (Australian, as well as foreign entities such as the UN) assumed a leading role. It was recognised that, if the local security situation deteriorated beyond the ability of the organisations already on the ground to deal with (e.g., AFP personnel), the military would have to redeploy personnel to get control of the situation. This need to quickly redeploy troops took place in both East Timor and the Solomon Islands in 2006.

Prior to 1998, the ADF had little interaction with the police. Before 1998, the AFP did not have significant experience or capacity for planning overseas operations. Importantly, the culture of the police was different from the military. The AFP personnel initially sent to these interventions were accustomed to eight-hour workdays as community policemen inside Australia, compared with the military norm of working the required amount of hours necessary to accomplish the mission. Whereas it was normal for the ADF to conduct detailed planning prior to and during an operation, the police were more reactionary, responding quickly to events as they happened (i.e., as they do when they receive word of a crime occurring).

In terms of the high-level management of the three operations outlined in this report, the ADF clearly led the initial planning and execution of INTERFET in East Timor. This was a potentially risky operation, where armed conflict could have broken out. Additionally, as will be detailed in Chapter Three, the situation was deteriorating rapidly in summer 1999; therefore, time was of the essence. In such circumstances, the ADF's considerable planning capability, as well as the fact that the overwhelming majority of Australia's initial response in East Timor was going to be military, made the ADF the appropriate choice as the initial lead agency. In the case of RAMSI, where there was considerably more time to plan prior to the intervention taking place, DFAT was well suited for the lead planning role. (It should be noted that while DFAT had more time to plan for RAMSI compared with the earlier operations, the ADF's operational-level planning time was short, roughly three weeks.) In the case of Bougainville and RAMSI, the ADF was in a supporting role to other agencies, namely DFAT and the AFP.

In addition to having relatively little experience working with other agencies in the Australian Government, the ADF of the late 1990s was not accustomed to playing a leading role in a coalition that included the military forces of several nations. From its earliest days, the Australian military has normally operated outside the country as part of a coalition, normally one led by either the United Kingdom or the United States. Beginning with the INTERFET intervention and continuing throughout the period examined in this report, the ADF was the leading member of these multinational military missions.

Australian Federal Police

In early 1998, the AFP had roughly 2,790 personnel. At that time, the AFP focused mostly on domestic police issues, with special attention being given to preventing illegal immigration and the trafficking of illegal drugs. A few AFP personnel were deployed to locations, such as Cyprus, and later that year, a handful of AFP personnel were sent to Bougainville. The AFP was not yet a significant participant in overseas interventions.

In May 1999, the AFP was tasked by the Howard government to provide 50 members for the UN Assistance Mission to East Timor (UNAMET). UNAMET was to provide assistance to the local police and help oversee the upcoming referendum on whether East Timor would achieve autonomy. The AFP personnel started to deploy in June,[11] and it was the start of a much more significant role for the police in overseas operations.

Important organisational and cultural differences existed among the police and other agencies that were to play major roles in foreign interventions. According to several interviewees, at the start of this period, the AFP had an internal culture based on its internal police role in Australia. Prior to 1998, the AFP had little interaction with DFAT or the military; there had been little if any need for this. Because of

---

[11] Australian Federal Police, *Annual Report 1998–1999*, Canberra, Australia, October 1999.

its focus on police work inside Australia, the AFP entered this period with a distinct disadvantage in terms of its internal organisations and processes to plan for and manage protracted overseas deployments. Like DFAT, the police tended to earmark personnel for longer overseas deployments compared with the ADF; six- to 12-month deployments were normal for police.

The experience gained in the deployment to East Timor started the process of giving the AFP the experience it needed. By the time of RAMSI in 2003, the police were an early, major participant in the planning of the operation. Indeed, in the case of RAMSI, the police were to lead on the ground in the Solomon Islands, with the ADF in support. Certainly, this was a new and different role for the police. At its peak, roughly 200 AFP personnel were deployed to RAMSI in 2003–2004.

The rapidly increasing role of the AFP in overseas interventions resulted in both an increase in strength as well as new internal organisations. By June 2004, the AFP's strength was up to some 3,470 personnel. By July, it absorbed the Australian Protective Service, and the new total strength was now roughly 4,800 personnel, giving the AFP greater ability to support protracted overseas deployments compared with five years earlier. From an organisational standpoint, an important change took place in February 2004, when the International Deployment Group (IDG) formed. This new organisation gave the AFP a much-better capability to manage overseas operations and included some 500 personnel, with some from State and Territory police organisations.[12]

Australian Agency for International Development
Formed in 1974, AusAID functioned as a separate executive agency from 2010 until October 2013, when it was integrated into DFAT. At the time of the interventions described in this report, AusAID was managing assistance efforts in many countries in the region. For example, in 1998, AusAID's portfolio included a $227 million AUD aid

---

[12] Australian Federal Police, *Annual Report, 2003–2004*, Canberra, Australia, November 2004.

program for PNG, roughly $70 million AUD for Indonesia, and separate aid packages for Bougainville and the South Pacific. Compared with the other governmental agencies described in this report, AusAID was small. In 1998, the total number of employees was roughly 580, with about 60 of that number serving outside Australia.[13] (Although it grew considerably as an executive agency, with more than 2,100 personnel by June 2012, 823 of whom were serving overseas.)

In addition to being smaller than the other government organisations that played important roles in overseas involvement, AusAID's perspective was quite different. In recognition that many of the nations in Australia's region are poor and underdeveloped, AusAID adopted an incremental, long-term perspective typical of the development community. By the time of the 1998–2003 interventions, AusAID had been involved with counties in the region for many years. The agency's approach was based on the realisation that economic, political, and social development in the countries to Australia's north would require a lengthy effort, where progress would be measured over years rather than weeks or months. This was a different view compared with several other agencies, particularly the ADF, which tended to take a short-term approach to interventions.

The different perspective of AusAID manifested itself in a number of ways. One was the tour lengths and positioning of its overseas personnel. Like DFAT representatives stationed overseas, AusAID officials typically serve two- to three-year terms in a posting. Yet, many postings are less embassy-centric and require working in more-remote areas of developing countries, where local interaction and understanding is imperative to success. Additionally, AusAID was more comfortable in development work, the results of which take a long time to come to fruition because of the relatively underdeveloped nature from many of the countries in the region were starting. This was in contrast to other agencies that, from AusAID's perspective, expected significant local improvements to be made within a year or less.

---

[13] Australian Agency for International Development, *Annual Report 1998–1999*, Canberra, Australia: 1999, pp. 3–5, 13–14.

Although AusAID had considerable experience with the countries of the region, including, in some cases, detailed knowledge of the situation on the ground, in the opinion of some AusAID veterans, their organisation was not included early in the planning for interventions. This was an important omission from AusAID's perspective, since it would almost certainly be remaining for the long haul once an intervention was completed. Therefore, AusAID felt that it should have been included early in the planning process.[14]

The next three chapters of this report examine the details of how the Bougainville, East Timor, and Solomon Islands interventions were planned and conducted. In keeping with the primary goal of the report, we focus on how operations were organised, planned, and conducted from a whole-of-government perspective. The report concludes with a summary of important insights and lessons that could be useful for Australian operations of this nature in the future.

---

[14] Interview with former senior official, August 2015.

CHAPTER TWO

Bougainville

Australia was compelled to eschew a policy of regional nonintervention and play a lead role in a multinational peace operation in its immediate periphery in Bougainville (Figure 2.1) in the late 1990s.[1] Bougainville had long been a source of separatism but, in the interest of maintaining amicable relations with the government of PNG, Australia tended to steer clear of intervening in such issues. By 1997, however, influenced by a destabilising course of events typified by the Sandline crisis and the public outcry domestically and throughout the region, Australia elected to change its policy approach. Shortly after a truce was reached between the government of PNG and Bougainvillean separatists in October 1997, a New Zealand–led Truce Monitoring Group (TMG) was deployed within roughly seven weeks, comprising military and police personnel from New Zealand, Australia, Fiji, and Vanuatu, as well as a contingent of Australian civilians.[2]

The signing of the Lincoln Agreement on January 23, 1998, augured the transition from the TMG to the Peace Monitoring Group (PMG) in May and shifted lead-nation status to Australia. Initially led by Australian Brigadier Bruce Osborne, the PMG endured until mid-

---

[1] The contributing information in this chapter was derived from Australian Government reporting, open-source research, and interviews conducted by the authors during a research trip to Australia in August 2015.

[2] Richard Fairbrother and David Lewis, "Unarmed Peace Monitors and Post-Conflict Situations: Practical Lessons from the Bougainville Peace Process," *International Governance and Institutions: What Significance for International Law?* 11th annual meeting, Wellington, New Zealand: July 4–6, 2003.

Figure 2.1
Bougainville

RAND *RR1556-2.1*

2003. The goal of the TMG and PMG was to ensure that the commitments made by both sides in the conflict were sufficiently being met. To do this, a network of permanent sites, manned by a combination of civilian and military representatives from the contributing regional states, was established throughout the island, supported by an interagency-headquarters element. Because the UN had established a political office to support the peace process, a handful of UN staff were present to serve as trusted interlocutors, chair meetings, and provide an added air of legitimacy. At its height, the PMG had 300 personnel located at six permanent sites. This was eventually reduced to 195 personnel, and then, following the signing of the Bougainville Peace Agreement in late August 2001, was cut to 75 personnel in three permanent locations.[3] The PMG ceased operations at the end of June 2003 and withdrew completely on August 23, 2003.[4] During the course of the six-year operation, the TMG/PMG cycled through 21 three-month civilian rotations, with an additional 2500-plus members of the ADF deploying.[5]

Planning and Preparation

Devising a Truly Unique Deployment

Given that the initial TMG was formed and deployed fewer than two months after the truce agreement, time for planning was at a premium. While it was clear from the outset that the Bougainville operation was going to involve an interagency footprint, it was, at the time, more comfortable to maintain a military lead. This was, after all, the first time Australian civilians would be taking part in such a deployment, and Defence was the only bureaucratic entity that could provide the necessary planning skills as well as logistical and support capabilities the mission would require.

Although the question of who would lead the Bougainville mission was not contested, some of the specific parameters were more hotly debated. Chief among these was the question of armaments. The BRA, the primary separatist faction, was wary of Australia's objectivity, as evidenced by its refusal to take part in peace talks in 1994, which were to be protected by the ADF under Operation Lagoon. Given the political sensitivities, it was understood in Australia, especially among DFAT, that arriving armed would be a problem. DFAT and the Department of the PM&C were also aware and supportive of the need for a

---

[3] Fairbrother and Lewis, 2003.

[4] Fairbrother and Lewis, 2003, p. 20.

[5] Stefan Knollmayer, "A Share House Magnified," *The Journal of Pacific History*, Vol. 39, No. 2, 2004, p. 221.

more-extended presence.[6] Within Defence, however, was a desire for a brief mission with an explicit exit strategy. There was also resistance to deploying the ADF with both unarmed military and with civilians in tow as a formal part of the mission. Ultimately, the question was resolved by a Cabinet-level decision after a DFAT representative argued the case and eventually convinced their Defence colleagues.

With trust for the Australians low and rumours about the true intentions of the regional contingent rife, the absence of weapons helped the PMG convince the Bougainvilleans that they were not an invading force.[7] Agreeing to go into Bougainville unarmed was nevertheless a huge risk for the ADF and was contrary to the military's internal culture. One former senior official stated plainly that CDF General John Baker "really put his reputation on the line" and "went against the advice of some colleagues and international allies."[8] It also did not help that Francis Ona, the self-proclaimed president of an independent Bougainville, delivered public and private threats to the PMG.[9]

Yet, the BRA initially resisted the agreement to take part in an operation unarmed. In fact, at the outset of the TMG in late 1997, the BRA refused to sanction the participation of ADF uniformed personnel (though civilian personnel from Defence were acceptable). It was not until after the initial rotation of personnel that enough trust had been built to allow for ADF participation to include the eventual taking over of the leadership role from the New Zealand Defence Force (NZDF).

With the weapons issue resolved, officials planning for the operation understood that the sensitivities of the local population would remain high. Despite efforts to quell cynicism, Australia had played a key role in building the capabilities of the PNG Defence Forces, and

---

[6]   Anthony Regan, "Light Intervention: Lessons from Bougainville," Washington, D.C.: United States Institute of Peace, 2010, p. 70

[7]   Fairbrother and Lewis, 2003, p. 12.

[8]   Interview with former senior official, August 2015.

[9]   Bob Breen, *Struggling for Self Reliance: Four Case Studies of Australian Regional Force Projection in the Late 1980s and 1990s*, Canberra, Australia: Australian National University Press, 2008, p. 118.

care had to be taken to make its neutrality evident. This was addressed by the adoption of two primary tenets: Maintain a small footprint and follow a clear mandate. Referring to personnel numbers in the context of local questions about Australian motives, a senior civilian official argued, "Bougainville was as light a touch as we could get away with. No one else was going to do it but we were, politically speaking, the least appropriate country to lead it."[10] The TMG/PMG mandate was also kept basic. Personnel were to maintain visible neutrality at all times, a policy that helped inspire the wearing of bright yellow T-shirts and caps. Personnel also were to provide proof that the political-military agreements agreed to by the opposing sides were being observed.

A former senior AusAID official raised a complaint about the planning process for Bougainville. According to the official, in the years prior to the TMG/PMG, AusAID traditionally had the most interest and was more active throughout PNG, especially with its outlying islands, than other Australian agencies. According to the official, DFAT was never that interested, and any military and police efforts were focused almost solely on training their PNG counterparts. Yet, despite having perhaps the best understanding of the local culture and politics of Bougainville, this official felt that it could at times be difficult for AusAID to be heard.

Pre-deployment Preparation for Personnel

Considering the unprecedented disposition of the Bougainville operation, it is notable that those who either led or otherwise took part in the TMG/PMG—be they military or civilian—generally laud the pre-deployment preparation they received. A senior military official involved in the earlier stages of PMG noted that the force preparation for peace monitors in Bougainville "would be a best practice as the Australian reps came well-prepared."[11] A civilian official who deployed on two occasions likewise felt that the pre-deployment training was excellent, notably the focus on cultural sensitivity, citing historian and

---

[10] Interview with senior official, August 2015.

[11] Interview with former senior official, August 2015.

then–Lieutenant Colonel Bob Breen—the director of training for the PMG—as being particularly skilful at working with civilian officials who were not well versed or experienced in working with the ADF.

Among some of the more-senior members of the PMG, pre-deployment preparation seems to have been adequate, although less formalised. A former senior military official remarked that their preparation was "reasonable," but that it was largely done independently by reaching out to previous commanders in Bougainville and that nothing was institutionalised.[12] There also appear to be some inconsistencies in the training provided to PMG personnel who served later in the mission. In an after-action report authored by Brigadier C. P. Appleton, commander of the PMG from December 2001 to June 2002, it is noted that, "Early in my tour, many incoming staff, particularly officers, were arriving disconsolate because they had received as little as a week's notice of their deployment."[13] It was not indicated whether such a lack of forewarning was due to more fundamental issues, such as the strain on the force of maintaining persistent rotations. Nevertheless, it signals that, at least for some, the requirement to get replacements in place in some cases trumped thorough preparation.

Implementation: A Limited Mandate, but with Gaps to Fill

Avoiding Culture Shock and Sustaining Effectiveness

Successfully carrying out the multinational, multiagency TMG/PMG operation required all of those involved to adapt to a mix of national and bureaucratic cultures on the fly. Each of the established patrol sites was staffed by civilian and military personnel representing numerous regional governments and agencies living in close quarters. In such an environment, periods of adjustment and instances of discord are unavoidable, although among interviewees, there was no mention of

---

[12] Interview with former senior official, August 2015.

[13] C. P. Appleton, "Post Operational Report: Operation Bel Isi II," copy of document provided to authors, June 2002b, p. 6.

any fundamental risk being placed on the mission as a result of this posture. Epitomising this arrangement, the senior civilian official who served as a deputy commander, known under the PMG as the Chief Negotiator, had living quarters adjacent to the military commander, and they worked in the same office. This subtle yet important detail was cited as a key factor in fostering coordination and building relationships throughout the TMG/PMG staff.

Crucial to the effectiveness of the mission was the inclusion of numerous regional partners. The Pacific Island contingent was key in Bougainville, as it brought a unique cultural and linguistic perspective that allowed many of their representatives to quickly build a rapport among the local population. The New Zealand contingent also included a number of ethnic Maoris who had similar successes. Yet, while the PMG mission gradually evolved into a "reasonably capable ad hoc regional peacekeeping organisation," it still faced a number of challenges related to the commingling of differing cultures.[14]

As late as July 1998, three months after the establishment of the PMG, issues with monitoring operations and morale remained apparent. Interestingly, in his seminal work on the Bougainville operation, Breen (whose training program was praised by an early civilian volunteer to the TMG) attributes much of the internal friction and insensitive behaviour regarding political and cultural issues to poor personnel selection and inadequate pre-deployment training on the part of the Australian and New Zealand contingents. An obvious part of the problem, he writes, was the disorganised transition from the TMG to the PMG, typified by the fact that "no Australians who had served with the TMG were invited to brief the next rotation of personnel . . . on conditions in Bougainville."[15] While no description is provided about changes in training protocols from late 1997 to mid-1998, this critique could be weighted toward an aforementioned lack of notice about deployments as well as a failure to utilise those personnel who had returned from deployments in pre-deployment exercises.

---

[14] Breen, 2008, p. 119.

[15] Breen, 2008, p. 119.

General Personnel Issues

Aside from inconsistent perceptions on the quality and time devoted to pre-deployment training, two other issues generally related to personnel management are commonly mentioned as challenges to the Bougainville mission. First, it was commonly noted among interviewees that sustaining a cohort of qualified and experienced civilians over time became a challenge for the respective Australian agencies. Senior government officials from Australia and New Zealand initially responsible for the Bougainville peace process were experienced in the Pacific and PNG, and they were effective in large part due to the personal relationships they had built during some of the pre-1997 peace efforts.[16] Such quality of personnel permeated into the earlier days of the TMG/PMG mission when, according to interviewees, there was a certain allure to volunteering for a tour in Bougainville. After a while, however, "it lost its lustre, and we had a lot of junior people with little to no professional experience taking part."[17] Another former senior military official concurred, crediting much of what they felt was the early success of the operations to having quality personnel: "We were getting the cream of the crop of volunteers. This became tougher later in the mission."[18] This concern was exacerbated by the second personnel issue mentioned: the length of deployment.

For the majority of volunteers to the TMG/PMG, deployments lasted only three to four months. This was largely because attracting civilian volunteers for overseas deployments required making some accommodations. It was also impacted by the fact that the contributing agencies were resource constrained and would find it a struggle to do without qualified personnel for longer durations. Such justifiable reasons notwithstanding, short deployments still presented TMG/PMG leadership with a persistent challenge. As Fairbrother and Lewis contend, key appointments often transitioned at around the same time, "undermining continuity and credibility. Hard-won trust and confidence was often lost. Relationships often needed to be built

---

[16] Regan, 2010, p. 81.

[17] Interview with former senior official, August 2015.

[18] Interview with former senior official, August 2015.

from scratch."[19] On the other hand, more-frequent turnover meant that, on rare occasions where a key relationship was not functioning properly, any damage was only short term.[20] A senior military official with experience in Bougainville reinforced this. While acknowledging that three-month civilian rotations made it tough to build continuity, they maintained that "bad eggs" were easy to move around.[21] Finally, in his post-operational report following command of the PMG, Brigadier Appleton argues, "Tenures of three months do not allow a Commander sufficient time to become highly effective."[22]

Interagency Planning and Execution

Incorporating and De-Conflicting Development and Assistance Efforts

Another aspect of the TMG/PMG operation that engendered varying perspectives among interviewees was the success with which Australia interwove its bilateral interests on Bougainville with those of the multinational mission. This was most apparent as it pertains to development efforts and other economic assistance. As discussed, the mandate for the PMG focused acutely on observing the peace and did not include development goals. Adhering to this limited objective at times posed a challenge for TMG/PMG leadership. A former senior civilian official mentioned the need to avoid "mission creep" in these types of operations. He also noted that he and his military counterpart worked together to ensure that some site leaders, mostly junior officers, did not deviate from this by providing aid to the communities to which they were assigned.[23]

Donor funding was provided with the best intentions to support and help facilitate the peace process, but it led to some unforeseen negative consequences. Anthony Regan, constitutional lawyer specialising

---

[19] Fairbrother and Lewis, 2003, p. 17.

[20] Fairbrother and Lewis, 2003, p. 17.

[21] Interview with former senior official, August 2015.

[22] Appleton, 2002b, p. 8.

[23] Interview with former senior official, August 2015.

in conflict resolution, identifies four primary funding categories that, in due course, proved to be flawed:

1. the funding of small-scale projects, often referred to as "peace dividends," awarded to communities that supported the peace process
2. allowances and other financial benefits provided to Bougainvilleans that made possible their attendance at peace meetings
3. payments made mostly by the UN, but also other donors, to facilitate customary reconciliation ceremonies (although not for items that could be exchanged for compensation)
4. financial incentives, typically in the form of small projects, for groups of former combatants to participate in a weapons management program in need of a jumpstart in 2001.[24]

The adoption of the term *peace dividends* introduced connotations that economic benefits were tied to the process, while, over time, many Bougainvilleans would not take part in peace process events without being provided with some form of recompense. Finally, incentives related to the weapons program initiated intense competitions among groups and led to a perception that funds were unevenly distributed. Perhaps most damaging was the collective tendency to view these benefits as primarily advantageous to Bougainvilleans with the closest connections to the international contingent.[25]

Australia's development efforts in Bougainville, which predated TMG/PMG by a number of years, would remain under the purview of AusAID. Yet, in the interagency environment generated by the peacekeeping mission, a reassessment of existing programs and goals would be undertaken and these programs would be subject to persistent reviews going forward. As one senior civilian official noted, development efforts were closely intertwined and coordinated with the efforts of the PMG. Thus, providing some of its personnel to peace monitoring, AusAID also had to manage development programs under

---

[24] Regan, 2010, pp. 82–83.

[25] Regan, 2010, p. 83.

timelines designed to enhance the status of the TMG/PMG, which included some short-term efforts that were anathema to how the organisation typically operated.

A former senior AusAID official recalled instances of bureaucratic disagreement about the substance and timing of development projects in Bougainville during the TMG/PMG years. Eager to demonstrate success in a mission whose mandate provided few opportunities for tangible progress, TMG/PMG leadership looked for and emphasised aid efforts to the underdeveloped island. Some AusAID officials, many who had more experience working on Bougainville than their inter-agency counterparts, bristled at being pressured to complete projects they felt were more cosmetic and did not contribute to a comprehensive long-term vision they preferred to develop. At various points, Defence and DFAT expressed frustration at the pace of development efforts, although AusAID pushed back. There was also an element of pressure coming from Bougainvilleans who wanted to take full advantage of the additional resources being committed. One resistance leader reportedly uttered, "Now there is peace, where is our hospital?"[26]

Much of the dissonance between Australia's development community and senior TMG/PMG officials (and, by extension, Bougain-villeans) stemmed from a fundamental misinterpretation of how aid resources are best used. AusAID, like other similar agencies, preferred to incorporate a strong understanding of local dynamics in devising a wide-ranging plan of development that prioritised capacity building carried out over a longer period of time. The officials affiliated with TMG/PMG, on the other hand, tended to view AusAID and the resources they brought as a means of inducing cooperation from the local communities. According to a non-AusAID civilian who served in the PMG, "The development guys were the money guys."[27] A former senior military official expounded, "AusAID field officers in Bougain-ville were 'gold nuggets' that could help mould and shape operatives and provided a huge source of leverage."[28] Given this outlook, it should

---

[26] Interview with senior official, August 2015.

[27] Interview with senior official, August 2015.

[28] Interview with former senior official, August 2015.

not be surprising that, to Bougainvilleans, development was the aspect of the Australian presence that was going to "pay off the most."[29]

It is important to note that, among interviewees outside the development community, the disparity regarding aid utilisation appears to be based on genuine misunderstanding. Impressions of AusAID personnel involved in Bougainville were overwhelmingly positive. The same senior military official who likened AusAID officers to "gold nuggets" praised, "Their [the AusAID staff's] understanding of local customs and religions as well as where other non-government organisations [NGOs] were operating was also very valuable."[30] The official also could not recall any philosophical disagreements with AusAID staff, noting that they were pragmatic and easy to work with. Thus, it is not apparent that those outside the development community fully comprehend what a former senior AusAID official declared, "The objectives of diplomacy and objectives of development are very different and operate on distinctly different timelines."[31]

Interest Wanes on the Part of the Security Forces

The ADF had reservations about deploying to Bougainville and in conjunction with civilian officials with whom they would closely work with on the ground. Despite taking over the leadership of the PMG in April 1998, Defence leadership in Canberra was reportedly eager to withdraw ADF forces from Bougainville early on. Brigadier Bruce Osborn, appointed as the first commander of the PMG in April 1998, felt that CDF Baker and Commander Australian Theatre, Major General Jim Connolly, "were overly focused on extracting the ADF from Bougainville as soon as possible, and handing the task over to DFAT and . . . AusAID."[32] Osborn felt that this desire to extricate the ADF as soon as possible was preventing the achievement of a whole-of-government approach he felt the mission needed.[33] Regan

---

[29] Interview with senior official, August 2015.

[30] Interview with former senior official, August 2015.

[31] Interview with senior official, August 2015.

[32] Breen, 2008, p. 118.

[33] Breen, 2008, p. 119.

argues that pressure from senior levels of Defence to facilitate a quick exit contributed to ADF commanders on the ground at times pushing the bounds of the agreed-upon division of responsibility and becoming heavily involved in dealing with local parties.[34] Although the question of the timing of a military withdrawal created some turbulence early in the mission, the ADF would ultimately continue to devote personnel and remain in command of the PMG until its conclusion in 2003.

The AFP initially provided volunteer personnel to the TMG/PMG effort, but after a few rotations had some misgivings about its participation. A senior police official stated that the AFP did not feel that its officials were being used in a way that best suited Bougainville. And although there were just one or two officials reporting to the J2 (Intelligence) staff and an additional six to eight AFP members who were part of the general contribution, in 2000, the AFP pulled out all of its AFP representatives from the PMG. Consequently, while the AFP would remain engaged with PNG in some of its police capacity-building initiatives, its personnel did not play a role in the bulk of the PMG mission.

By 2002, among concerns that Bougainville leadership was growing too dependent on the PMG for such areas as transportation, mediation, and weapons disposal, the relevant Australian agencies reached a general consensus that it was the right time to plan for a withdrawal.[35]

Intelligence Support

Throughout his time in the operational theatre, Brigadier Osborn criticised the lack of intelligence support he received from the Defence Intelligence Organisation (DIO), the Australian Theatre Joint Intelligence Centre (ASTJIC), and Office of National Assessments (ONA) in Canberra. Brigadier Osborn reported that he was "basically having to operate in an information vacuum" because of the fact that his command was "seeing virtually no reporting on Bougainville from DIO, ONA, and ASTJIC."[36] This is relevant not only because it placed limi-

---

[34] Regan, 2010, p. 68.

[35] Regan, 2010, p. 70.

[36] Breen, 2008, p. 120.

tations on the TMG/PMG mission, but also because it is indicative of a recurring theme throughout the interventions examined in this report.

Issues Related to the End of the Mission

The signing of the Bougainville Peace Agreement in August 2001 paved the way for a three-part path forward: weapons disposal, autonomy, and a referendum on the political future of the island. The primary task of the PMG in 2002 and 2003 was to help facilitate the first of these pillars.[37] Moreover, the added stresses placed on the civil service and military from the onset of the East Timor crisis in 1999 and, subsequently, participation in the broader war on terrorism following the attacks of September 11, 2001, diminished the priority of the operation.[38] Thus, Canberra looked to reduce commitments in places that were not of prime strategic significance, and Bougainville found itself in the crosshairs of a resourcing squeeze.

In the case of the PMG, it is apparent that concerns other than the conditions on the ground in Bougainville influenced the timing of its conclusion. Rather than setting a hard completion date, however, Canberra's preference appeared to be whittling personnel down until ending the mission became imperative. A former senior military official stated that Foreign Minister Downer was informed at some time that Bougainville was reduced to the point that the next move would be to take everyone out. Another former senior military official felt that it was clear that Major General Peter Abigail, then the Land Forces commander who oversaw the PMG, had difficulty maintaining broad support for the mission among officials in Canberra.

In regard to an exit strategy, one former senior civilian official argued that the speed of the developments in Bougainville in 1997 necessitated a reaction that led to the rapid deployment of the cobbled-together TMG. Thus, Australian officials did not spend a lot of

---

[37] Natascha Spark and Jackie Bailey, "Disarmament in Bougainville: 'Guns in Boxes,'" *International Peacekeeping*, Vol. 12, No. 4, Winter 2005, pp. 599, 601.

[38] Knollmayer, 2004, p. 225.

time planning toward desired conclusions. As they summed it up, "We didn't have an entry strategy, so how could we have an exit strategy?"[39]

Conclusion and Lessons

The Bougainville operations from 1997 to 2003, although conducted in small numbers and in a permissive environment, proved a formative event in Australia's transition to a whole-of-government approach to carrying out complex overseas interventions. In a bureaucracy that is relatively small, the TMG/PMG years provided the opportunity for a new generation of civil servants and military personnel to interact in a way that would enhance future operations where the stakes were higher and the risks greater. Bougainville's impact could be seen concretely on future operations; as one interviewee pointed out, "Three of five members of my Bougainville team ended up in more senior positions during RAMSI."[40] Another senior civilian official noted that the Bougainville experience helped DFAT work in an interagency environment and in particular get to know the ADF better.

The TMG/PMG is generally viewed as a successful operation, although it would be a mistake to credit this to flawless organisation and implementation, as other factors were at play. Among the Bougainvilleans, it worked because of the timing and the fact that people had grown tired of persistent violence and a collapsed economy. The mission also benefitted from individuals who were able to succeed, despite some deficiencies exposed in deploying and supporting personnel abroad, issues that Australia struggled with in East Timor. As Breen argues, "Formal processes for Australian military force projection had been too slow. It had been ad hoc arrangements between internal coalitions of willing staff at the tactical level within the ADF and NZDF, as well as the PNG section at DFAT, that had delivered these impressive results."[41] Having to rely on the personal relations and initiative of the

---

[39] Interview with senior official, August 2015.

[40] Interview with senior official, August 2015.

[41] Breen, 2008, p. 104.

individuals tasked with carrying out a mission in lieu of institutional capabilities, while perhaps more dependable in a smaller bureaucracy, incurs greater risk and should be minimised.

In the context of the Bougainville intervention, there were a handful of issues that, if better managed at the institutional level, would have been beneficial to the whole-of-government nature of the mission. First, it is clear that more could have been done in the planning stages to incorporate the knowledge of AusAID personnel who, prior to the TMG, were more active in Bougainville than any other Australian Government agency. Additionally, the evidence suggests that the notification time for those deploying as part of the TMG/PMG, particularly among ADF personnel, was short and negatively impacted preparation. Relatedly, it is clear that the opportunity to leverage the experiences of returning TMG/PMG personnel in the training of subsequent rotations was missed. Finally, the research revealed the aforementioned conceivable positive note when it comes to short rotations. Nevertheless, the net cost of lost continuity and compromised local legitimacy implies that, even if they remain a necessity, senior policymakers should incorporate the effects of these quick turnarounds into their plans and expectations.

At a more operational level, the key takeaway from Bougainville is that fostering sustainable stability in an underdeveloped region is a time-consuming effort that offers few, if any, shortcuts. Even introducing seemingly minimal incentives and allowances can, as demonstrated, build dependencies and have a strategically negative impact. Segregating the mandates of the TMG/PMG with that of AusAID's development efforts may have been the most-appropriate division of labour, but the lack of a comprehensive understanding of how the latter operated led to avoidable points of friction. For a mission essentially focused on passively validating that an agreement was being adhered to, the allure of a robust aid program to show progress and maintain the support of the local communities is understandable. However, expectations among some Australian officials not affiliated with AusAID nor familiar with how the agency typically functioned proved to be misguided. Among a number of lessons cited by Brigadier Appleton, one in particular stands out:

A Western-style desire to get quick results, often by paying a relatively small premium financially, must be balanced against the fact that in all subsequent financial dealings the same premium or greater will be expected. The belief in third world countries that those from the first world have unlimited resources is well nigh unshakable.[42]

---

[42] C. G. Appleton, "Lessons Learned Bel Isi II," internal Australian Government report provided to authors, June 10, 2002a, p. 2.

CHAPTER THREE

East Timor/Timor-Leste

Despite coming after the start of the Bougainville operation, Australia's participation in INTERFET is widely viewed as the catalyst that thrust the bureaucracy into a more contemporary approach with regard to regional and international stability and security.[1] According to one former senior military official involved with INTERFET, this operation marked an important transition from the post-Vietnam "doing nothing" mindset—largely adopted by policymakers who came of age in that generation—to a new willingness to partake in military operations all over the world.[2] East Timor (Figure 3.1) was the first time Australia served in a lead-nation status for a large multinational operation, which meant it had to incorporate more agencies and allies into its planning. And as one former senior official noted, more agencies bring more complexity and demands to make things work seamlessly. Coordinating with NGOs, engaging in civil-military issues, and leading allies all made for something difficult and different. A number of deficiencies of some existing capabilities and processes, particularly within the Australian military, were exposed in this transition. INTERFET, however, served as a watershed event that introduced a new era of whole-of-government coordination that would enable Australia to become involved with and, in some cases lead, a number of multinational operations in the region and across the globe.

---

[1] The contributing information in this chapter was derived from open-source research and interviews conducted by the authors during a research trip to Australia in August 2015.

[2] Interview with a former senior official, September 2015.

Figure 3.1
Timor-Leste

The 1999 INTERFET mission was the result of a widespread security crisis throughout East Timor following an independence referendum that was sanctioned by the Indonesian government. In the aftermath of the vote that overwhelmingly supported independence, pro-Indonesian government militias, with the implicit or even direct support of the Indonesian military, engaged in widespread reprisal attacks against communities who elected to secede. UNAMET, which was established with the approval of the UN Security Council to help the East Timorese plan for the referendum and subsequently conduct it, comprised only about 1,000 personnel, made up of principally civilians and police as well as 50 unarmed military officers; it was unable to address the rapidly escalating violence.[3] International outcry, especially from Australia, the United States, and Portugal, led to Indonesia's support for a UN-sanctioned and Australian-led peace enforcement mission under Chapter VII of the UN Charter.[4]

Planning for Australia's Most-Significant Deployment Since Vietnam

As developments on the ground in East Timor developed rapidly and as the situation grew more precarious, INTERFET had to assemble and plan quickly. A former senior military official classified it as essentially a bridging operation for the subsequent UN mission, the UN Transitional Administration in East Timor (UNTAET). At the operational level, the ADF was clearly in the lead because of the unpredictable security situation and the need for short-notice planning, an area where the military is particularly well suited. This impacted the level of interagency and multinational involvement in the planning, as military leaders had to complete plans in a time frame that limited the ability to include allies and other government agencies in the process. Nevertheless, at the strategic level, in 1999, Canberra would see the existing bureaucratic coordinating mechanisms function in new ways as well as the establishment of a variety of different ministerial and interdepartmental entities. These entities were established to focus exclusively on planning for and implementing the East Timor intervention.

---

[3]   Michael G. Smith, "INTERFET and the United Nations," in John Blaxland, ed., *East Timor Intervention: A Retrospective of INTERFET*, Melbourne, Australia: Melbourne University Press, 2015.

[4]   United Nations, "Chapter VII: Action with Respect to Threats to the Peace, Breaches of the Peace, and Acts of Aggression," undated.

Storm Clouds on the Horizon: Shaping the Bureaucracy Prior to INTERFET

Although the INTERFET operation was not formally approved until September 1999, a number of circumstances were at play that provided forewarning to Australian officials that a military-focused deployment to East Timor could be in the offing. First was the request by Indonesian President Bacharuddin Jusuf Habibie to the UN in January 1999 that it hold an independence referendum in East Timor. The following month, the NSC issued a proposal for increased readiness for the ADF, fuelled largely by concerns that Australian citizens would have to be evacuated from East Timor or other strife-prone areas in the region. DFAT, however, was in favour of relying on diplomacy to address any impending crisis and voiced concerns about how the Indonesians and Timorese would perceive overt Australian military preparations. In what is one of the few widely documented interagency disagreements from the period, Minister of Defence John Moore, after consulting with Prime Minister Howard, elected to "ignore DFAT's concern and agree to CDF Admiral Chris Barrie's recommendation to proceed with readiness planning and consultation with U.S. Pacific Command."[5] A former senior military official substantiated this, noting that the ADF, at least at senior levels, saw fit to engage in broad preliminary planning for a contingency under UN auspices shortly after the Habibie announcement. And, while the Australian planning process for what would become INTERFET was described as "very much ad hoc," the fact that the ADF had the better part of a year to work through the issues ultimately made it manageable.[6]

The NSC proposal also appears to have influenced other agency and interdepartmental adjustments among Australia's national security policy community. Though wary of the optics of heightened military preparedness, DFAT, for its part, likewise understood the need to devote more resources to the burgeoning issue and established an East Timor Task Force led by Nick Warner early in the year. In April, CDF Barrie, foreseeing the significant role the UN would play in any even-

---

[5] Connery, 2010, pp. 24–25.

[6] Interview with a former senior official, September 2015.

tual operation, appointed then–Brigadier Michael Smith to the new position of Director-General East Timor. Along with various representatives from DFAT and AusAID, Smith travelled regularly to New York and served as a key interlocutor with the UN Department of Peacekeeping Operations.[7] Also in April, a new committee was added to the interdepartmental policymaking structure, led by Bill Paterson, an assistant secretary in PM&C. The group comprised representatives of equivalent positions from DFAT, Defence, AusAID, the AFP, the Australian Electoral Commission, and ONA, and met fortnightly to discuss developments in East Timor and related overseas issues (although never military operations). According to an official familiar with the committee, this seemed to be a productive way to bring PM&C back into the fold, as it was not explicitly responsible for any facet of the operational planning.[8]

Collectively, these efforts comprise the major preliminary modifications that would assist the Australian Government in preparing for and, in some cases, managing the events that eventually unfolded in East Timor. As things evolved, however, a second wave of bureaucratic refinement would subsequently be ushered in, as the hope of the ballot for Timorese independence gave way to wanton violence and intimidation.

Looming Crisis: Preparing for Peace Enforcement

There were signs that the situation in East Timor was deteriorating as 1999 progressed. In June and early July 1999, media reports, complaints from members of the recently deployed UNAMET mission, and reports from Australian liaisons attached to the UN depicted an increasingly dire situation as pre-referendum intimidation by anti-independence gangs gradually broadened.[9] Such accounts made it clear that a military-heavy peacekeeping or peace enforcement effort, which

---

[7]   Chris Barrie, "Creating an Australian-Led Multinational Coalition," in John Blaxland, ed., *East Timor Intervention: A Retrospective of INTERFET*, Melbourne, Australia: Melbourne University Press, 2015.

[8]   Connery, 2010, p. 28.

[9]   Breen, 2008, p. 130.

the Indonesian government had hitherto rebuffed, was likely. In fact, when UN Resolution 1264 sanctioning INTERFET was formally approved in mid-September 1999, it provided a clear mandate with broad authorisations for the peace-enforcement force that would carry it out.[10] The three primary directives were:

1. Restore peace and security in East Timor.
2. Protect and support UNAMET in carrying out tasks.
3. Within force capabilities, facilitate humanitarian assistance operations.

Importantly, the UN Security Council authorised INTERFET to *take all necessary measures* to fulfill these mandates.[11] At the strategic level, adjustments were made at the NSC that would subsequently impact how its subordinate elements functioned, in particular SCNS and SPCG, as well as the general management of the crisis once it commenced.

At the start of the Howard administration in 1996, the NSC had been structured such that it comprised six of the senior-most policymakers tied to national security portfolios (the Prime Minister, Deputy Prime Minister, the Foreign and Defence Ministers, Treasurer, and Attorney General) and five senior officials who, if necessary, could be called to provide information and guidance on a specific topic (the Secretaries of PM&C, DFAT, and Defence; the Chief of Defence Force; and the Director General of ONA). As the East Timor crisis escalated in 1999, this protocol was altered such that officials and even relevant ministerial advisers would regularly attend NSC meetings. This reportedly brought more structure to the proceedings and, by permitting more senior officials to hear and even participate in the entire debate, promoted a better general understanding of strategic thinking. As CDF

---

[10] United Nations, Security Council, "Resolution 1264 (1999)," September 15, 1999.

[11] Alan Ryan, "Primary Responsibility and Primary Risks: Australian Defence Force Participation in the International Force East Timor," Duntroon, Australia: Land Warfare Studies Centre, November 2000, p. 25.

Barrie recalls, "The great benefit was we all knew just what part of the jigsaw puzzle was being played with at the time."[12]

Unsurprisingly, however, this procedural change consequently affected the roles played by the SCNS and SPCG. As the NSC process evolved and boasted an ever-expanding participant list, the traditional SCNS members were increasingly incorporated into NSC meetings, especially once they started meeting on a near-daily basis. In essence, the crisis-management process that emerged in 1999 saw no distinct role for SCNS because "in the crisis's acute phase, because the overlap in membership between the senior committees and the fast pace of events made SCNS redundant."[13] SPCG, on the other hand, remained active and was valued for its ability to bring together senior officials (at the Deputy Secretary and equivalent levels) at short notice and its ability to be action oriented. Nevertheless, some officials were critical of SPCG for achieving a level of collegiality that made it vulnerable to "groupthink" as well as its inability to "be anything more than where a discussion took place."[14]

Largely taking the place of SCNS and SPCG was a committee created by Prime Minister Howard and led by Alan Taylor, who had recently been appointed head of the Australian Secret Intelligence Service and had previously served as a Deputy Secretary at PM&C and the ambassador to Indonesia. The "Taylor Committee," also referred to by some as the East Timor Task Group, was an ad hoc body tasked with coordinating national policy and reporting on policy development to the NSC. It was made up of two components: a small secretariat of middle-ranking officials seconded from DFAT, Defence, Immigration, AusAID, and PM&C; and more-senior officials representing their departments and agencies at daily committee meetings.[15]

Although the ADF had time to engage in general planning for East Timor, only a few key personnel were involved from the outset.

---

[12] Connery, 2010, p. 9.

[13] Connery, 2010, p. 138.

[14] Connery, 2010, p. 13.

[15] Connery, 2010, p. 39.

Due largely to concerns about leaks to the media, once an intervention of some type appeared all but imminent, CDF Barrie restricted planning for INTERFET to a handful of senior officials within Defence, called the Strategic Command Division (SCD).[16] CDF Barrie initially planned the strategic and operational aspects of the East Timor mission in cooperation with his Head of SCD, Major General Michael Keating. By early August, then–Major General Peter Cosgrove was brought into the top-secret compartment of the SCD, where he integrated the tactical elements.[17] The close relations of these three architects of the effort and a tendency to hold tight lines of communication would continue into the onset of the INTERFET mission. Finally, later into the contingency planning process, CDF Barrie formed an organisation within the SCD, known as the INTERFET Branch, to serve as a strategic coalition manager and liaise with DFAT in identifying and subsequently negotiating with and managing potential coalition partners.[18]

September 1999 also saw within Defence the formation of another new task force at the direction of CDF Barrie. The East Timor Policy Unit (ETPU) was charged with pooling expertise and focusing the department's policy work. Barrie, explaining his logic, stated, "Basically, we needed our own mini-SPCG."[19] At its height, the unit comprised roughly 12 analysts from across Defence; its two senior officers, Mike Scrafton and Peter Jennings, were promoted to First Assistant Secretary so that this mini-SPCG could operate on a 24-hour basis during the crisis. An added benefit of the unit was that its limited membership helped to prevent leaks about the planning process. The secretive nature of the initial planning phases notwithstanding, as the situation in East Timor became increasingly dire, other elements of the Australian bureaucracy became more involved. When the violence started, the CDF called a planning meeting and, according to one

---

[16] Breen, 2008, p. 131.

[17] Breen, 2008, p. 133.

[18] Connery, 2010, p. 37.

[19] Connery, 2010, p. 36.

former senior official, "The government snapped into place."[20] Overall, however, the IDETFs were assessed as "pretty messy and ad hoc" by one former senior official.[21]

As the situation in East Timor got more tense, lower echelons of command could ascertain from news reports and official announcements that an intervention was becoming increasingly likely. For example, in July, both Foreign Minister Downer and Minister of Defence John Moore hinted publicly at Australia's intentions. Though not formally directed to do so, elements of the Australian Army began preparations for a deployment that looked increasingly likely. This spurred a disjointed, multi-echelon planning process that, as Breen argues, "Was informed by the media; not by the chain of command or intelligence."[22]

Taking place in a tense and unpredictable environment with a host government only dubiously supportive of the peacekeeping force, the INTERFET operation was heavily centred on the military and was straightforward in nature. Then–Major General Cosgrove envisioned a four-phase, detailed campaign:

1. Negotiate with Major General Kiki Syahnakri, Indonesia's appointed Chief of the Martial Law Authority in East Timor, for a safe arrival and quartering for Australian personnel.
2. Rapidly deploy as many combat forces as could be facilitated.
3. Establish a secure environment, first in Dili, then throughout East Timor.
4. Transition INTERFET to a UN peacekeeping force.[23]

While the character of the INTERFET mission necessitated a heavy initial focus on security, other factors contributed to the Australian military playing a prominent role. As one former senior military official noted, at the time, the Indonesian government was heavily influenced by its senior military leaders. As a result, Australian mili-

---

[20] Interview with former senior official, August 2015.

[21] Interview with former senior official, August 2015.

[22] Breen, 2008, p. 132.

[23] Breen, 2008, p. 139.

tary representatives, be they attachés based in the Australian Embassy in Jakarta or senior officials visiting from Canberra, had traditionally played a more-active role in diplomacy with the Indonesians than they typically would if Australia had been dealing with another country. For instance, months before the referendum, attaché staff maintained open lines of communication with their Indonesian counterparts. Then–Brigadier Jim Molan, a Defence attaché at the Australian Embassy in Jakarta, met regularly (each evening when in East Timor during this period) and had a close relationship with Jackie Anwar, the Indonesian military's "man on the ground" in East Timor.[24]

Facing Hard Realities and Enduring the Paradigm Shift

In 1996, the NSC establishment signalled a new recognition that responsibilities for overseas contingencies were spread broadly across the Australian bureaucracy. The experience in East Timor would substantiate this. Although INTERFET began as a predominantly military operation, other government agencies would play a prominent role in East Timor, both as part of this mission and especially during the follow-on UNTAET, which focused on preparing East Timor for independence in 2002. Increased involvement by DFAT and the AFP would foster adjustments in the ways each agency typically operated. One former senior official stated that, at the time of East Timor, Australia was just starting to move out of a single-agency mindset in favour of thinking more in terms of a whole-of-government approach, a system for which the evolving NSC was designed. Another senior official at that time concurred, saying that, for the first time, the Australian Government system, via the NSC mechanism, shifted the senior political levels to a mode in which they could request and "pull things" from the bureaucracy. Optimising this system, however, took time and required some initial adjustments.

---

[24] Interview with former senior official, conducted on July 23, 2015. Transcript provided to the authors on September 28, 2015.

Australian Defence Force and the Challenge of Implementing INTERFET

Although the planning for the INTERFET mission was initially restricted to a handful of senior military officials, as preparations began in earnest, it was clear that aspects of its implementation would prove problematic. One former senior official recalled that, prior to the operation, when asked by Prime Minister Howard how the military would deploy, CDF Barrie candidly replied, "with great difficulty."[25] At the strategic level, Australia had a clumsy command and control process at the time that, according to one senior military official, had to be quickly discarded in favour of reliance on personal relationships among military leaders. As a former official later noted, "We made things work despite the command and control systems we had [which was] built on the idiocy of the Defence of Australia concept from the mid-nineties."[26] While speaking more charitably, David Connery nevertheless concurs, stating, "The intervention into East Timor further showed the need to reconsider Australia's defence policy after a long period dominated by the Defence of Australia concept."[27]

Other challenges quickly became apparent at the operational level as well. As Governor-General Sir Cosgrove would recall years later, the respective services that comprised the ADF were tactically proficient but resource constrained and inexperienced in certain key warfighting functions, such as supplying large, remote operations, conducting high-tempo transport operations over long distances, and supporting a land operation. In sum, argues the INTERFET commander, "'Jointery,' the application of joint warfare techniques, was a crude and infant art in the Australian Defence Force in 1999."[28]

Other fundamental capabilities were absent as well. For instance, one interviewee shared an anecdote that the Australian Army had dif-

---

[25] Interview with former senior official, August 2015.

[26] Interview with former senior official, conducted on July 23, 2015. Transcript provided to the authors on September 28, 2015.

[27] Connery, 2010, p. 137.

[28] Peter Cosgrove, "Commanding INTERFET," in John Blaxland, ed., *East Timor Intervention: A Retrospective of INTERFET*, Melbourne, Australia: Melbourne University Press, 2015.

ficulty acquiring enough fresh water for the initial deployment and was forced to send personnel into the city of Darwin to buy all the bottled water they could. This contributed, continued the interviewee, to the harsh reality that Australia struggled with deployments in its own backyard: "We had a Brigade-minus in East Timor and had to beg, borrow, and steal to sustain it for six months."[29] This reality reportedly had a significant impact on the Cabinet. And while the first response was anger, it eventually set in that these difficulties were symptomatic of an Army that had been reduced as a result of years of cuts and was not prepared for a major overseas deployment. As one former senior official bluntly offered, "In essence, it was a third-rate defence force trying to carry out a fourth-rate mission."[30]

Interagency Coordination Turns the Corner

Since INTERFET was primarily a security, peace enforcement–type operation, there was no Australian senior civilian official or co-lead assigned. This was in part driven by the fact that, although Australia provided roughly half of the 11,500 military personnel (a figure representing the peak strength in late 1999), 22 nations contributed to INTERFET. Thus, there was concern that if one senior Australian civilian was assigned to the command, most, if not all, of the other contributing nations would have sent senior civilian representatives as well. As a former senior military official put it, such a "glut of civilian plenipotentiaries" would have made things in East Timor much more convoluted.[31] Another former senior defence official stated that, when the INTERFET mission started, the relationship between DFAT and ADF was "tense."[32] It soon became apparent that, while the rushed planning for INTERFET had created some interagency challenges, the working relationship on the ground among the various organisations helped make the mission a success.

---

[29] Interview with former senior official, August 2015.

[30] Interview with former senior official, August 2015.

[31] Interview with former senior official, August 2015.

[32] Interview with former senior official, August 2015.

Although no senior civilians were formally part of the INTER-FET mission, a former senior civilian official stated that they returned to East Timor to re-establish consular duties in Dili roughly a week after then–Major General Cosgrove and the INTERFET forces landed. Despite not being tied to the coalition, the civilian official kept in regular contact with the military component, speaking with General Cosgrove daily. It was also helpful that General Cosgrove's chief of staff served with the senior DFAT official on a previous deployment to Bougainville. Additionally, the DFAT official spent a lot of time with General Cosgrove's senior civilian advisor from Defence, who was well versed in the political-military arena but less familiar with the local culture and customs.

The only potential source of interagency discord mentioned in interviews regarded reporting from East Timor back to Canberra. A former senior military official conveyed that an official from DFAT wanted to provide separate reporting to a committee in Canberra, but "had the decency" to share his plans with the military command. To maintain uniformity of reporting, it was agreed that the command would review all transmissions and any disagreement was thus avoided.[33] One former Army officer describes the situation:

> I'm not sure the extent to which I had visibility on the reporting back to Canberra, though I never felt that multiple lines of communications back to Canberra led to misperceptions there. We also had a blizzard of visitors from Canberra, which made staying on message easier.[34]

In the run-up to INTERFET, the military attachés in the Australian Embassy in Jakarta maintained regular contact with senior Indonesian officials and communicated frequently with relevant officials in Canberra. According to one former senior official familiar with the situation, attachés in Jakarta spoke almost daily with General Cosgrove

---

[33] Interview with former senior official, August 2015.

[34] Interview with former senior official, August 2015.

prior to his arrival as well as with the DFAT-led crisis centre, the CDF, and even the Prime Minister.

Australian Federal Police Evolves into a Deployable Force

No agency underwent more of a transformation as a result of the change in Australian overseas intervention policy than the AFP. The AFP had never been part of the national security community until the late 1990s and, according to one interviewee, prior to the early 1990s, it was essentially described as "cops on a beat."[35] While the AFP were not key players in INTERFET, the organisation had personnel dedicated to all three East Timor missions. After the transition to UNTAET, the AFP quickly found itself playing a more-intensive role. With only a small deployment as part of the UN mission in Cyprus as precedent, the AFP had to quickly adapt to working abroad in larger numbers, sustaining successive deployments, and coordinating among elements of the Australian interagency community with which it had little, if any, track record.

At the institutional level, the AFP was increasingly becoming involved in a domain that was traditionally in the exclusive purview of DFAT and Defence. During this period of adjustment, according to a former senior official, the AFP tended to be a passive player in Canberra and found itself in somewhat of a subordinate position. It was a bit overwhelmed about taking on a new position, and when AFP personnel deployed, their guidance was essentially, "Don't rock the boat, do what you're told."[36] Additionally, the police culture of this period was not oriented toward overseas deployments nor was the AFP well versed in the bureaucratic cultures of DFAT, AusAID, or the ADF.

At the operational level, calibrating the AFP organisation to sustain overseas deployments posed a particularly bedevilling challenge. One senior police official bluntly declared, "East Timor hit us in the face."[37] The number of AFP deployed as part of UNAMET was described by a senior police official as a "handful" that increased to

---

[35] Interview with former senior official, August 2015.

[36] Interview with former senior official, August 2015.

[37] Interview with senior official, August 2015.

about ten under INTERFET. In UNTAET, however, AFP numbers grew quickly: from ten to 50 in roughly the first three months, from 50 to 80 in the three months after that, and finally peaked at around 100 three months after that. The AFP at this time was not structured for these missions, and it was soon a strain to have persistently deployed 100 AFP to East Timor in the 1999–2001 time frame. One fix at the time was to extend the length of deployments from three to six months.

Tactically, the AFP reportedly experienced some issues engaging locals in East Timor. Considering the culture of the organisation prior to East Timor, it is not surprising that language skills and cultural knowledge were in short supply. Thus, growing pains were apparent and, as one former senior official put it, "There was a bit of the 'ugly Australian' happening."[38]

Fixing Intelligence

As mentioned, INTERFET revealed a number of government systems in need of improvement in order to meet operational requirements. One institutional function that underwent a fundamental change during this period was intelligence. According to one former senior official, prior to INTERFET, Australian intelligence was exclusively focused at the strategic level and not designed to support operational or tactical units. Broader questions designed to inform senior policy-makers, such as, "What's going on with China?" were prioritised.[39] With forces deploying to an unpredictable foreign environment, it was apparent that this would need to change. Yet, once again, the transition encountered some bumps along the way.

While there was not yet a pattern of "pushing" intelligence down to lower echelons, the location of the mission brought some benefit in this regard. According to one official involved in East Timor, Australia enjoyed two distinct advantages at the outset: (1) good knowledge and understanding about the local landscape that helped facilitate informed decisionmaking and (2) excellent language skills among a handful of officials assigned to both Indonesia and East Timor, which

---

[38] Interview with former senior official, August 2015.

[39] Interview with former senior official, August 2015.

allowed for valuable rapport building among both Indonesian officials and the East Timorese. Thus, having a cadre of bureaucratic officials well versed in the language and culture and with strong contacts within the Indonesian government proved valuable.

During INTERFET, the intelligence community for the first time began pushing reporting down to units who needed it, not just briefing the Prime Minister and the Cabinet. Several interviewees commented on both the strengths and weaknesses of the intelligence support for INTERFET. It was noted that there was a need to coordinate the passing of intelligence among agencies that were not used to this dynamic. In particular, the intelligence arrangements for this operation were a new experience for the AFP, which had to make some organisational adjustments to deal with the intelligence products it was now expected to assimilate. For example, early in INTERFET, the police did not have sufficient numbers of personnel with the required clearances who could access the intelligence products.

The Importance of Clear Messaging and Guidance

Fundamentally, INTERFET's mandate was straightforward and clearly understood in the Australian Government: Establish a secure environment and transition authority from a UN peace enforcement to a peacekeeping force under UNTAET. Beyond that, however, it is apparent that more-nuanced guidance from senior levels in Canberra was often lacking, leaving the leadership on the ground in East Timor to work out some of the details of the mission based on their interpretation of Canberra's goals. Part of this may have been due to the trust placed in INTERFET's commander. As one interviewee familiar with the operation offered, "Cosgrove was a big personality who increasingly had the ear of the PM [Prime Minister]."[40] Indeed, a former senior official noted in an interview that, when detailed guidance to deal with a situation was lacking, a statement was written and sent to Canberra with the message: "If you don't instruct differently, this is the protocol

---

[40] Interview with former senior official, August 2015.

that will be followed."⁴¹ While there was no formal statement from Canberra, the perception there was that those on the ground grasped the intention of the Australian Government and, given this, the leadership in Canberra was comfortable with this assertiveness.

In general, the level of explicit guidance from Canberra was limited during INTERFET. A former senior military official stated that the government in Canberra gave the ADF considerable latitude in how to conduct the mission. General Cosgrove stated, for instance, that General Keating, was his main point of contact in Canberra, and although he was in communication with Canberra, the interaction consisted of "just chats, nothing more formalised."⁴² This was, in many respects, appropriate, but framing and communicating instructions from senior levels in Canberra could have been more thoroughly executed. For instance, a political-military directive, provided by Defence with DFAT input, was mentioned as something that would have been preferable to having to engage in some level of speculation. Another area in which high-level guidelines were lacking was with regard to border protocols along the frontier between East Timor and Timorese Indonesia, a particularly precarious issue at times. Too often, operational- and tactical-level personnel were left to deal with a tense situation without the benefit of strategic-level guidance to fall back on.

Another key area where the theatre command was not afforded specific direction was in its engagement with Indonesian officials. With a history of amicable relations, Australian military officials worked hard "not to create lasting damage with the Indonesians" while carrying out their mandate.⁴³ Senior Australian military officials on the ground in East Timor reportedly spoke with their Indonesian counterparts frequently but were never asked or required to provide reports to Canberra or the Australian Embassy in Jakarta. Additionally, neither Canberra nor the embassy provided agenda recommendations or shaping instructions for senior military officials to use during these communications. It is apparent that more could have been done to ensure

---

⁴¹ Interview with former senior official, August 2015.

⁴² Interview with former senior official, August 2015.

⁴³ Interview with former senior official, August 2015.

the intended messages were reaching the relevant interlocutors on the ground as well as to keep the leadership and officials in Canberra better appraised of what was happening in the country.

The lack of guidance from Canberra also may have contributed to the stove piping of information among only a handful of senior military officials. Corroborating General Cosgrove's point about communicating primarily with General Keating, another former senior military official explained the latter's influence on the lines of communication. According to that source, General Keating effectively ran the INTERFET mission from Canberra, in that General Cosgrove reported directly to General Keating, who then only reported directly to CDF Barrie.

Later in the operation, after the security situation became more settled and other aspects of the Australian bureaucracy became more involved in East Timor, a lack of detailed guidance and consistent messaging played a role in some frictions with the local leadership as well. José Ramos-Horta, initially the influential spokesperson of the Timorese movement and later the first foreign minister of Timor-Leste, was an active interlocutor who spoke fluent English and politicked aggressively with the United States and the UN to pressure Australia to get involved in East Timor. Once the independence of East Timor was established, the new government wanted to establish its own voice and, in the process of doing so, the dynamic of the bilateral relationship with Australia shifted. Despite this, there remained a lack of a clearly articulated and unified policy on the part of Australia to guide the increasing number of officials who were in regular contact with counterparts in East Timor. According to a former senior civilian official, Ramos-Horta attained standing among numerous senior leaders in Canberra and was gifted at capitalising on gaps in Australia's messaging. If he was unsatisfied with the answer he received from the force commander or a diplomat on the ground, he could call Foreign Minister Alexander Downer directly.[44] In essence, evidence suggests that, while the trust and independence bestowed upon General Cosgrove during the tenuous days of the INTERFET mission succeeded in lieu

---

[44] Interview with former senior official, August 2015.

of precise strategic guidance from Canberra, the de facto sustainment of this condition during a more-normalised peacetime environment made for a more muddled situation.

Return of the ADF in 2006

In late April 2006, violence once again erupted in Timor-Leste, this time fuelled by long-simmering discontent within the Timorese defence forces. The immediate trigger of the crisis was the dismissal of nearly 600 soldiers from the Forças Armadas de Libertação Nacional de Timor-Leste (FALINTIL)/Forças de Defesa de Timor-Leste (F-FDTL), otherwise known as the "petitioners," who were from the west of the country and had protested perceived discrimination by senior officials from the east.[45] With UN peacekeepers no longer present in the country, it quickly became apparent that an outside force would need to be inserted to help restore order. With a large number of its citizens and strategic interests in Timor-Leste, the ADF would once again be sent.

In the run-up to the 2006 crisis, Australia was increasingly less engaged with Timor-Leste. After leading the INTERFET operation and playing a significant role in the follow-on UNTAET mission until its conclusion in 2002, with the transition to independence, the aforementioned cracks in the bilateral relations between Australia and Timor-Leste were more pronounced. By 2004, Timor-Leste was less of a priority for Australians in general, as other contingencies—such as the RAMSI mission, Afghanistan, and Iraq—were ongoing or steadily gaining prominence. At higher levels of the government, these more-active theatres forced Timor-Leste down the list of priorities. Australian involvement was further impacted in May 2005, when the successor to UNTAET, the UN Mission of Support in East Timor (UNMISET), formally concluded, removing the last of the international peacekeep-

---

[45] Cynthia Brady and David Timberman, "The Crisis in Timor-Leste: Causes, Consequences and Options for Conflict Management and Mitigation," Washington, D.C.: United States Agency for International Development, November 2006, p. 1.

ers. Thus, when it was time to respond in 2006, Australia was caught somewhat off-guard and was lacking some of the situational awareness it previously was able to maintain.

As in 1999, the security situation in 2006 in Timor-Leste was highly unpredictable. Then–Brigadier Michael Slater, the commander of the responding Joint Task Force 631, argued in an interview after the deployment that, "The situation that we faced in the first 5 days here this time was, in some significant ways, more complex and uncertain than the situation we faced in 1999."[46] Some of the lessons of 1999, however, would come into play.

There is also evidence that, in the intervening years since the start of INTERFET, the ADF was able to make progress in improving some of its obvious deficiencies revealed by the initial deployment. According to Brigadier Slater, the reinsertion of ADF personnel in 2006 fared much better from a sustainment standpoint:

> Since INTERFET, we have poured resources into rectifying the problems we had . . . sustaining ourselves away from our Australian bases . . . We have put around 2500 people into this theatre and sustained them superbly.[47]

Despite this, then–Brigadier Slater felt there were still some improvements to be made, particularly regarding personnel management. Stressing the importance of cultural and linguistic knowledge, Slater notes, "We have a reservoir of people with Tetun skills and experience in East Timor, but the personnel system cannot identify them in a hurry when we are deploying."[48] This is particularly important when deploying to a semi-permissive environment, where clear communication can mean the difference between a tenuous episode being defused and an incident detrimental to the mission.

---

[46] Mick Slater, "An Interview with Brigadier Mick Slater," *Australian Army Journal*, Vol. 3, No. 2, Winter 2006, p. 10.

[47] Slater, 2006, p. 11.

[48] Slater, 2006, p. 14.

Apparent improvements to the deployment capabilities of the ADF notwithstanding, the dynamics leading up to the resumption of violence in Timor-Leste reveals that Australia still had work to do to achieve a whole-of-government posture that was comprehensively focused on the environment in which it was operating. Perhaps most significant was the common refrain among interviewees that Australian officials were generally unaware that the situation in Timor-Leste was about to deteriorate so drastically.

At the macro level, this was largely seen as a product of waning Australian engagement. One interviewee suggested that Australia felt the Timorese government had grown too ungrateful. Policymakers in Canberra decided to "let them [the Timorese government] sort it out themselves" when it began pulling its personnel out in 2005. At the time of the crisis, the official estimated that there were only six ADF advisors remaining in Timor and argued that "we dropped the ball on intel as well."[49] Another former senior official felt that, by 2006, there was no Australian entity left in Timor that was focused on local politics. Instead, DFAT had become overly focused on the "big politics" of the UN and national-level entities, which prevented the detection of the impending escalation stemming from more localised grievances.

A senior DFAT official conveyed that a review of Australia's development efforts in 2006 revealed two primary shortcomings: (1) there was an evolutionary approach to development with no formal strategy put in place, and (2) no one saw the 2006 crisis coming. A former senior military official pointed out that the dispute was essentially between the Timorese military and police; the development of both forces was supported by Australia. Despite this, "We didn't really understand what was going on."[50] In this case, however, shorter deployment durations of three to four months, particularly by the AFP, were seen as a main culprit that undermined capacity-building efforts as well as situational awareness.

---

[49] Interview with former senior official, August 2015.

[50] Feedback from a former senior official on an early draft of this report, provided on February 2, 2016.

In summing up the situation, a former senior official argued that, while Australia was able to overcome some early hurdles to make INTERFET a success, "we screwed it up on the other end."[51] Continuing, they cited "a lack of experience, foresight, and strategic thinking" that contributed to the timing of the initial reduction of Australian resources and helped pave the way for the 2006 crisis. Another former senior official critical of the withdrawal from Timor felt that there was also a degree of wishful thinking at play among Australian leadership, who overestimated the resilience of some of the changes that had taken place.

Conclusion and Lessons

Not unlike Bougainville, the Australian interventions in East Timor from 1999 to 2006 are viewed as general successes, although more to the credit of competent and motivated individuals and less on institutional efficiency. As Breen concludes in his chapter on INTERFET, "Based on its outcomes, the intervention was an outstanding success. Based on its processes, there was much for the ADF to reflect on."[52]

Importantly, the clear and limited mandate of INTERFET meant that the end state for the operation was more lucid than in Bougainville and the Solomon Islands. As a former senior military official simply summed, "We will not leave until the UN troops and officials could re-enter safely."[53] It also helped that roughly 70 percent of the forces in place at the conclusion of INTERFET donned blue berets as they transitioned to the follow-on UNTAET mission.[54] Despite this, INTERFET demonstrated to Australian officials that, while an intervention led and organised by a single entity may make things simpler and minimise leaks of information, it might not be the most effective or efficient option. As a former senior civilian official pointed out, "Quickly into

---

[51] Interview with former senior official, August 2015.

[52] Breen, 2008, p. 148.

[53] Interview with former senior official, August 2015.

[54] Smith, 2015.

the INTERFET mission, we learned that it was expensive to conduct ADF-only type missions."[55] A former senior military official took the same tone, offering, "A key lesson of INTERFET and Lagoon was that military planners should engage other agency planners as soon as possible."[56] William Maley, a DFAT official at the time, is critical about the lack of depth and breadth of inclusion in the preparation for INTERFET, stating, "Many staff in a range of federal government departments who should have been involved in high-level planning for the crisis which eventuated were otherwise occupied at the time when planning should have been at its height."[57] Even some of INTERFET's primary actors understood this and moved to make changes that would lead to more inclusive policy development. A former senior civilian official said that General Cosgrove, later while serving as CDF, had the command and control processes revamped and designed to better integrate a whole-of-government approach.

At the institutional level, a number of apparent deficiencies were tied to a fundamental dearth of specific guidance from multiple agencies and actors in Canberra. Australian officials on the ground in East Timor were not provided with a comprehensive political-military directive that ideally would have been issued by Defence with DFAT's input. Additionally, no direction was provided on how Australian officials on the ground should interact with their Indonesian counterparts, nor was any reporting of such interactions required by any agency in Canberra. Finally, a review of development efforts revealed that there was no overall strategy underpinning these activities. The appointment of strong, capable officials to carry out the mission and a lack of collective experience managing overseas whole-of-government efforts may have been contributing factors. Despite this, senior officials in Canberra should have been more assertive in deliberating on and articulating a more-inclusive strategic vision for East Timor.

---

[55] Interview with former senior official, August 2015.

[56] Interview with former senior official, August 2015.

[57] William Maley, "Australia and the East Timor Crisis: Some Critical Comments," *Australian Journal of International Affairs*, Vol. 54, No. 2, 2000, p. 159.

Aside from an insufficient strategic outlook, East Timor exposed other issues related to whole-of-government coordination. As with Bougainville, the intelligence reporting on East Timor during this period was inconsistent in quality, and measures were not in place to share all reporting across agencies. From a cultural standpoint, there was also a disconnect among the various government agencies about what kind of information was most useful. While perhaps understandable given the unprecedented nature of the mission, as will be seen, these issues persisted in future similar operations. Intelligence reporting covering in-depth political dynamics in Timor-Leste also suffered a setback, as the bilateral dynamic of the relationship evolved and other international priorities took centre stage. In time, the number of Australian officials lessened, and the respective agencies involved in Timor-Leste became increasingly focused on their own priorities at the expense of coordination. This contributed to a breakdown in situational awareness that prevented Australian officials from recognising the warning signs that led to the 2006 security crisis.

A prominent feature of Canberra's response to East Timor from a bureaucratic perspective was the formation of a number of interdepartmental (as well as intradepartmental) emergency task forces to better focus on the crisis as it evolved. Before assessing the utility of these, however, it is important to note that, for the most part, these were relatively short-lived. While there was indeed a hectic span of four to six weeks beginning in early September—recall that, in an extreme case, Defence's E1PU functioned around-the-clock—by late October, many task force members returned to their previous work or were assigned to serve on the East Timor desk in their respective agency. Due at least in part to this, for the most part, the efficacy of these committees has escaped scrutiny. The lone exception is the Taylor Committee, which in effect replaced SCNS and SPCG, and for which opinions on the utility of the group were mixed.

The Taylor Committee was formed at the behest of Prime Minister Howard and reportedly reflected a desire to streamline policy advice and address the Prime Minister's concerns about the efficiency of interdepartmental coordination. Prominent among the critics were General Keating and Hugh White, who, as Deputy Secretary for Strategy and Intelligence, Defence, served as a member of both the SCNS and SPCG. According to General Keating, "If you don't like the output, [leaders should] tell SPCG to create the right output, rather than create another body."[58] White agrees, arguing that the creation of the Taylor Committee "was a mistaken move and a move that was made more about bureaucratic politics than good advice to government."[59] On the other hand, Michael Scrafton, who served as the director of the ETPU, was of a contrary opinion. He stated, "The whole support to government stepped up eight or ten notches as a consequence of Allan's committee."[60]

The interventions in East Timor, more so than the lower-profile Bougainville operation and in conjunction with global events, ushered in a new collective attitude throughout the Australian bureaucracy about how a whole-of-government approach to overseas operations can help in pursuing strategic interests. Though ad hoc in much of its implementation, the collective impact of INTERFET was profound. As a former senior military official claimed, "We are now 1000 times better at operations than we were then. We were very clumsy, but we got through it."[61] Writing years later, then–CDF Barrie argues, "INTERFET marked a major shift in the way Australians had been thinking about their defence force—if they had thought about it at all . . . the experience of INTERFET was building a sound base that we would end up working from in meeting the array of challenges the following years would bring."[62] As a former senior civilian stated, "In only four years, we went from a 20th-century mindset into a more-complex 21st-century one," arguing that East Timor led to a new era of defence spending and investment and changed the political environment, which was key.[63] Referring to the ad hoc, yet impres-

[58] Connery, 2010, p. 100.

[59] Connery, 2010, p. 100.

[60] Connery, 2010, p. 100.

[61] Interview with former senior official, September 2015.

[62] Barrie, 2015.

[63] Interview with former senior official, August 2015.

sionistic nature of the operation, another former senior civilian official remarked, "East Timor was an example of a complete intervention on the run, but we got quite good at it."[64] They also noted that this impacted planning for the RAMSI mission in 2003. Damien Kingsbury, a journalist and academic specialising in the politics and security of Southeast Asia, concurs, noting that this was helped by the public support that accompanied the operation, "The political popularity of INTERFET in Australia, along with ongoing instability in the region, also led the Australian government to more assertively promote its regional presence, notably in the Regional Assistance Mission to Solomon Islands (RAMSI) from 2003."[65] The next chapter examines this next regional intervention in greater detail.

---

[64] Interview with former senior official, August 2015.

[65] Damien Kingsbury, "The Strategic and Political Consequence of INTERFET," in John Blaxland, ed., *East Timor Intervention: A Retrospective of INTERFET*, Melbourne, Australia: Melbourne University Press, 2015.

CHAPTER FOUR

Solomon Islands

For most of the 21st century, Australia has played a leading role in regional efforts to stabilise the Solomon Islands (Figure 4.1). While by far the most prominent and longest lasting of these commenced in 2003 as RAMSI, it was in 2000 that Australia first took part in a peace-monitoring effort on its periphery and in cooperation with a multinational contingent.[1]

In mid-October 2000, the Townsville Peace Agreement delivered a respite from four months of near anarchy following the coup that removed Solomon Islands Prime Minister Bartholomew Ulufa'alu. This paved the way for the establishment of a regional International Peace Monitoring Force (IPMT), a team comprising 35 Australian and 14 New Zealanders, as well as a smaller representation from Vanuata, Cook Islands, Tonga, and other Pacific states.[2] As in the Bougainville operation, the members of the IPMT were unarmed and explicitly neutral. Unlike in Bougainville, however, the Townsville Peace Agreement was, in the words of a senior civilian official, a "stop-gap" that was ultimately unsuccessful in resolving the underlying issues facing the country.[3] Importantly, of the 143 people who attended the peace negotia-

---

[1] The contributing information in this chapter was derived from Australian Government reporting, open-source research, and interviews conducted by the authors during a research trip to Australia in August 2015.

[2] Jeni Whalan, "Security and Development: Australian Experiences of Peacekeeping and Peacebuilding in Solomon Islands," report delivered at a conference, January 2012.

[3] Interview with official, August 2015.

Figure 4.1
Solomon Islands

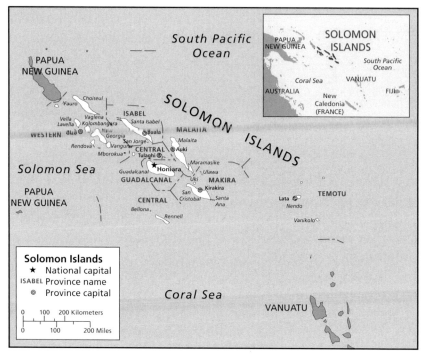

NOTE: Honiara is administered as a province-level town. It also serves as the capital of Guadalcanal Province.

RAND RR1556-4.1

tions, none represented the Solomons' influential women's or religious groups nor the prominent militia leader Harold Keke.[4]

Ultimately, the IPMT dissolved in June 2002, after it was determined that no more could be done to restore peace. Due to a number of circumstances, however, the IPMT was unlikely to succeed in resolving some of the deep-seated political issues, but there is evidence to suggest that Australia was not in the best position to be effective. According to a civilian official, at the time of the IPMT establishment, resources in Australia were fairly limited, due in part to the mission in East Timor,

---

[4]   Whalan, 2012.

and there was not great political will to engage in the Solomon Islands. At the operational level, the IPMT mission also suffered from poor pre-deployment training for its participants.[5] This experience would, however, influence senior leaders in the run-up to RAMSI.

After years of adhering to a policy of intervening lightly, if at all, in the political spheres of its neighbouring Pacific Island states, many credit the attacks of September 11, 2001, as altering this mindset. Cautioning against an isolationist mindset in interacting with regional instability, an influential pre-RAMSI report on the state of the Solomon Islands proclaimed:

> Without an effective government upholding the rule of law and controlling its borders, Solomon Islands risks becoming—and has to some extent already become—a petri dish in which transnational and non-state security threats can develop and breed.[6]

It was in this environment that the Australian Government, led by Prime Minister John Howard "discovered an urgent imperative for neighbourly concern that eventually led to the formation of RAMSI."[7]

The nature of RAMSI was distinct from that of East Timor (with its clear disposition toward the military) and even Bougainville, where the "lightest touch possible" had to be implemented to account for local sensitivities. In this case, the Australian Government was responding to multiple requests by the government of the Solomon Islands to intervene in a persistently unstable environment. According to one interviewee, the thought of going to the Solomon Islands was not daunting but served as a sea change in the Australian approach to the South Pacific, where sensitivities about appearing neocolonial were traditionally high. It was also clear to those involved that this mission would

---

[5]   Knollmayer, 2004, p. 230.

[6]   Elsina Wainwright, *Our Failing Neighbour: Australia and the Future of the Solomon Islands*, Barton, Australia: Australian Strategic Policy Institute, June 2003, p. 13

[7]   Mary-Louise O'Callaghan, "RAMSI—The Way Ahead," in Sinclair Dinnen and Stewart Firth, eds., *Politics and State Building in the Solomon Islands*, Canberra, Australia: Australian National University Press, 2008, p. 186.

be decidedly more multifaceted than East Timor and more hands on than Bougainville.

By the time of RAMSI, there was clearer recognition that there was a need for early whole-of-government planning and that, in RAMSI, the ADF would be in support of DFAT and the AFP, rather than play the lead role as in the Bougainville and East Timor operations. One former senior military official stated that such a posture "[m]ade operational sense and no one questioned it, which was a sign of the maturity of our processes."[8] Another senior official argued that, by the time RAMSI came about, interagency improvements had been made: "We had deep policy debates and then made informed decisions."[9] Thus, the conditions were in place for an all-hands-on-deck type of intervention that was recognised by most, if not all, involved, and that the intervention would necessitate close interagency coordination. As a senior civilian official noted, "It was known at the outset that the mission would sink or swim based on coordination."[10]

At its peak in September–October 2003, the number of personnel dedicated to RAMSI reached about 2250, which included 1800 military (1500 of which were Australian), 300 police, and civilian advisers. By early 2006, the number of military, reduced due to early security successes, dwindled to a standing force of roughly 70. The Participating Police Force (PPF), at 288 personnel, maintained a rather steady stream of forces, roughly half of which were provided by the AFP. The civilian component, which initially included only about 40 advisers, grew to more than 100 by this time.[11]

It is notable that, at the time, RAMSI was not the only regional effort competing for Australian civilian personnel. Also in 2003, the Australian Government signed the Enhanced Cooperation Program with the government of PNG. According to one interviewee, the agreement would send roughly 50 Australian civil servants to operate

---

8   Interview with former senior official, August 2015.

9   Interview with former senior official, August 2015.

10   Interview with senior official, August 2015.

11   Michael Fullilove, "The Testament of Solomons: RAMSI and International State-Building," Sydney, Australia: Lowy Institute for International Policy, March 2006, p. 8.

directly in PNG government ministries. Finding willing and competent candidates to serve in these unique overseas capacities, one official involved in the process argued, would prove a huge challenge. Overall, however, the success of this was ultimately viewed as a positive in that the effort consolidated coordination efforts and engaged people at the most senior levels.

Unknown at the start of RAMSI was how long this new brand of intervention would last, particularly in terms of the ADF and AFP having to maintain personnel in the Solomon Islands. In July 2013, ten years after functioning as a whole-of-government effort, RAMSI transitioned to a police-only mission, with development efforts returning to a bilateral status within Australian and New Zealand aid programs. In that time, the Australian Government spent $2.6 billion AUD on the overall RAMSI mission, accounting for 95 percent of the mission's total cost.[12] It should be noted that AusAID had been operating in the Solomon Islands for years before the RAMSI operation took place.

Planning and Preparation for RAMSI

Engaging in a Whole-of-Government Planning Process

The planning for RAMSI was done in Canberra under the guidance of a task force led by DFAT and an Interdepartmental Working Group (IWG), run by PM&C. RAMSI is distinct in that it was the Australian Government's first attempt to initiate a foreign operation that integrated not only DFAT, Defence, and the AFP, but also "AusAID, Treasury, the Department of Finance and many other agencies."[13] According to one interviewee, PM&C had grown in influence in the post–September 11 period, which proved important because it could bring Defence through the interagency planning process better than DFAT. DFAT and Defence, it was noted, had existing rivalries, while PM&C had the clout to set an agenda.

---

[12] Jenny Hayward-Jones, "Australia's Costly Investment in Solomon Islands: The Lessons of RAMSI," Sydney, Australia: The Lowy Institute, May 2014, p. 2.

[13] Fullilove, 2006, p. 13.

Aside from the operational requirements involved, Australia's defence establishment was influenced by broader considerations in its support for relinquishing the principal role it assumed in East Timor and Bougainville. In the case of RAMSI, Defence reportedly pushed for DFAT (overall) and the AFP (for security on the ground) to be the lead agencies, as it did not want the military to become the course of first resort in the Pacific. It was generally recognised, however, that a show of military force would be required, particularly at the outset. One former senior civilian official argued that in this regard the precedent of the IPMT in 2000 "that didn't go well," influenced then–Major General Cosgrove to push for a big show of military force at the outset of RAMSI (as opposed to the "tiny footprint" from 2000).[14] Another former senior civilian official familiar with RAMSI offered a more detailed but slightly different account. According to this official, Defence was not enthusiastic about RAMSI and, when informed it had to go, insisted on an exit strategy. The ADF felt it was a police issue but ultimately understood its forces were needed for the "shock and awe" in the initial stages and for force protection.

As for leadership of the mission, the titular head of the RAMSI organisation, called the *Special Coordinator*, would be a senior DFAT civilian official. The AFP would be the lead agency for restoring rule of law and directly command the multinational PPF. With regard to military leadership, given the prominence of the operation, there were a number of brigadiers and colonels who wanted to command what would become Combined Task Force (CTF) 635. Given the size of the initial deployment, this may have been appropriate in a typical situation. In this case, however, senior ADF leadership realised that they would not be the lead element in the operation and were wary of having their personnel remain in the country longer than was necessary. Thus, it was decided that the CTF 635 commander would be a lieutenant colonel and, later on, at times, a major.

This was in line with the desire within Defence to keep a lower profile. As a former senior military official put it, Defence "did not want to make military prominence there a self-fulfilling prophecy by

---

[14] Interview with former senior official, August 2015.

making it too rank-heavy."[15] While having a mid-ranking officer in command of ADF forces may have been appropriate in comparison to the size of the force, a senior civilian official who served after the initial rotation disagreed. According to that official, it made for an awkward partnership with senior counterparts: "As I arrived, there was a one-star equivalent AFP commander and a major ADF commander. This didn't work."[16]

There were clear institutional planning distinctions concerning the resources available for the process and the timelines considered for the RAMSI effort. Guidance from General Cosgrove was to have the ADF's role reduced as soon as possible, within 60–90 days. The AFP, on the other hand, developed a phased ten-year plan for RAMSI to build police capacity. The ADF's time horizon was much shorter. According to several interviewees, police planning for RAMSI was comprehensive. For example, the AFP planned for several phases: (1) years 1–3, (2) within 5 years, and (3) years 5–10. Despite the improvements in AFP planning of the previous few years, one senior AFP official reflected that working with the ADF impressed upon them the degree of specialisation and professionalism the military dedicates to such efforts. In his post-operation report as first commander of CTF 635, then–Lieutenant Colonel John Frewen voices a similar point about institutional differences with regard to planning: "The AFP does not have a similar culture or language to the ADF for formal planning."[17]

In addition to DFAT, the ADF, and AFP, the Australian Treasury was part of the planning for the Solomon Islands. This was due to the fact that part of the crime in the Solomon Islands was government officials who signed off on cheques to criminals. Therefore, the government of the Solomon Islands requested that representatives from Treasury serve there to lend credibility and improve the process of managing government funds.

---

[15] Interview with former senior official, August 2015.

[16] Interview with former senior official, August 2015.

[17] John Frewen, "Combined Joint Task Force 635 Post Operational Report," copy provided to the authors, January 21, 2004, p. 4.

Pre-deployment Training and Preparation

Although the interagency community in Canberra was considering an intervention for some time, there was relatively short notice given to those who would implement the RAMSI mission at the operational level, as was the case with East Timor and Bougainville. The military leadership was only given roughly three weeks, while DFAT and the AFP had more notice, roughly ten weeks.

Despite the relatively short time to prepare for the deployment, the primary components of the RAMSI operation—the ADF, AFP, DFAT, and AusAID   were able to partake in a pre-deployment inter-agency rehearsal that was touted by the first commander of CTF 635. This event was described by then–Lieutenant Colonel, now–Major General Frewen as being "absolute gold dust" for its value in managing expectations among the agencies and helping to clear up some misunderstandings before getting on the ground.[18] In addition to the planning rehearsal, there was a pre-deployment reconnaissance to Guadalcanal. A senior ADF official stated that taking part in this was critical, as it provided a true sense of where they would be deploying. According to them, "We would've been blind otherwise."[19]

The value of the exercise notwithstanding, some of those involved in the initial days of RAMSI feel they would have benefited from a more-robust whole-of-government training period. Lieutenant Colonel Frewen wrote in his post-operational report that, while the pre-deployment training was "sufficient from a WofG [whole-of-government] perspective to meet the level of threat encountered in Honiara," he recommends, "In [the] future, there should be greater emphasis on integrated training between the ADF, AFP and DFAT."[20]

In addition to RAMSI providing a great lesson in interagency planning, this operation allowed the planners to be the initial implementers. Nick Warner, who would serve as the first Special Coordina-

---

[18] Russell W. Glenn, *Counterinsurgency in a Test Tube: Analyzing the Success of the Regional Assistance Mission to Solomon Islands (RAMSI)*, Santa Monica, Calif.: RAND Corporation, MG-551-JFCOM, 2007, p. 62.

[19] Interview with senior official, August 2015.

[20] Frewen, 2004, p. 5.

tor; Ben McDevitt, the initial leader of the PPF; and Lieutenant Colonel Frewen were all intimately involved in the planning of RAMSI from the outset.

A New Twist on Interagency Leadership: The Role of the Special Coordinator

With so many agencies partaking in the planning of the RAMSI operation, one detail that was reportedly overlooked for some time was what specific shape the leadership would take. According to a senior civilian official, it was only toward the end of the planning period, roughly two to three weeks prior to deployment, that it dawned on the planners that figuring out the mechanics of coordination on the ground was crucial. This was the time that DFAT representatives went around to other agencies to make the case for a Special Coordinator position and that the appointee would come from DFAT. This was agreed upon without considerable objection, given that Defence wanted to play a limited role, and the AFP, though a primary agency, had little track record of managing overseas missions. Nevertheless, the details of such an unprecedented position still needed to be worked out.

The variation of participants in the RAMSI mission precluded the appointment of an individual who could credibly hold command authority over every entity. Yet, so many moving pieces required a central figure to help ensure that the comprehensive objectives were being effectively pursued. Thus, as one senior civilian official pointed out, the directive for the Special Coordinator had to be delicately written such that the position held "all of the responsibility, none of the power."[21]

As described by a senior civilian official, the Special Coordinator was a high-level position negotiated among Defence, DFAT, and PM&C. Once the authorities were delineated, a letter signed by Prime Minister Howard was provided, outlining the Special Coordinator's responsibility to oversee, but not necessarily direct or command, the operation. As one of the early Special Coordinator appointees explained, "I essentially had a 'red card' that I could use to prevent something from happening that I felt would impede the mission, but

---

[21] Interview with senior official, August 2015.

I never had to use it . . . and didn't want to."[22] Another former Special Coordinator to RAMSI voiced the same sentiment, noting that they received a letter from Prime Minister Howard explaining their role, which made clear that they did not command the military or police, but did have them in support.

Though widely viewed as perhaps the best solution to the difficult question of leadership in a whole-of-government environment, the position of the Special Coordinator was not without some drawbacks. A former senior civilian official who served in RAMSI felt that the Special Coordinator position was, at times, a "difficult mechanism."[23] According to the official, there were some early difficulties in coordinating with the military, driven by differences of opinion regarding mission priorities and military capacity. Any friction was ultimately worked out in short order and ultimately did not adversely affect the operation, but it did provide an early test to the leadership model. Additionally, while not necessarily a fault of the position, its uniqueness made a certain level of on-the-job training inevitable. As one of the early Special Coordinators observed, "When I first arrived, the biggest thing that hit me was the amount of my time I had to devote to actual coordination, which was about 50 percent."[24]

As the RAMSI mission persisted, some interviewees pointed out a change in the seniority and experience levels of those who served as Special Coordinator in later years. The first two Special Coordinators, Nick Warner and James Batley, were senior and brought a great deal of local experience to the position. According to one senior civilian official, however, as time went on, the prominence of the Special Coordinator waned a bit, as the toughest aspects of the mission, namely restoring security, concluded. Relatedly, this seems to have impacted the level of control of the mission enforced by Canberra. While initially Nick Warner was given considerable autonomy to operate in the Solomon Islands, RAMSI's key coordination mechanisms centred on

---

[22] Interview with former senior official, August 2015.

[23] Interview with former senior official, August 2015.

[24] Interview with former senior official, August 2015.

Canberra and, as time went on, more-extensive controls were placed on subsequent Special Coordinators from the capital.[25]

Making It Work on the Ground: The Implementation of RAMSI

The RAMSI Treaty, signed in July 2003 between the government of the Solomon Islands and the key participants in the mission, provided the legal authority necessary to carry out the mission. This was a fundamental requirement to ensure all parties were on the same page and provide the operation with legitimacy. As a former senior civilian official noted, "Legislation was required for the operation so our mandate was clear. We had to be very careful to operate within our authorities."[26] In addition to the treaty and the well-defined leadership role of the Special Coordinator, guidance from Canberra was noticeably more detailed than it had been in either East Timor or Bougainville. One former senior Defence official noted that they believed RAMSI received more strategic-level guidance because it was the first time a civilian was in the lead.

By all accounts, instances of interagency disagreement were rare; when issues arose on the ground that could not be resolved, they were referred to the IWG in Canberra for solution. One example of this was the question of how to reinforce and provide security for the prison in Honiara (discussed in the next section). To provide a unified front, the three principal leads of RAMSI—Nick Warner, Ben McDevitt, and Lieutenant Colonel Frewen—would conduct town-hall meetings all over the country to engage the communities, explain the goals of the mission, and help allay any false rumours. Warner also travelled to the capitals of the coalition nations to keep them informed.

By all accounts, the initial show of force provided by the ADF was absolutely essential in conveying a message to those who would

---

[25] Jon Fraenkel, Joni Madraiwiwi, and Henry Okole, "The RAMSI Decade: A Review of the Regional Assistance Mission to Solomon Islands, 2003–2013," July 14, 2014, p. 76.

[26] Interview with former senior official, August 2015.

contest RAMSI: They would be met with stiff resistance. So as not to appear as an invading force, however, the ADF had to walk a fine line between maintaining a presence without appearing aggressive. Again, this was successfully completed. As a senior civilian official in the initial RAMSI deployment remarked, the military footprint was key. To demonstrate its capabilities in an unthreatening way, the ADF conducted some "open days," during which helicopters, military equipment, and weapons were on display as well as a demonstration of the capabilities of ADF's working dogs.[27] These went over well with the local population, as evidenced by an estimated 10,000 locals turning up for one such open day hosted in Honiara. Importantly, "It was a show of force, but not a scary force."[28]

Despite keeping the leadership of CTF 635 at the lieutenant colonel level, there were 52 majors initially assigned to it, making the command rank-heavy, given its size (a tongue-in-cheek alternative for the RAMSI acronym was "Recruit Another Major for the Solomon Islands"). None of these majors, however, attended Staff College and therefore did not know what a Combined Joint Task Force looked like or how it should function. Moreover, CDF Cosgrove ordered there would be only one lieutenant colonel in the command. Due to this restriction, the lieutenant colonel logistical battalion commander could not deploy and instead was replaced by his executive officer, a major.

Aside from the rank disparities, the rapid success of stability efforts made some other military staff extraneous. A former senior civilian official stated that, for some of the ADF, once law and order had been attained, the RAMSI staff had to find things for them to do. For instance, a psychological operations team that had never been to and did not particularly understand the Solomon Islands kept making proposals that were not culturally feasible. Many of these and other unnecessary personnel got cut within the first month or so. In addition, there was eventually an effort to bring in personnel with experience in Timor and Bougainville.

---

[27] Feedback from a senior official on an early draft of this report provided on January 21, 2016.

[28] Interview with former senior official, August 2015.

On the AFP side, lessons learned from the initial deployment of its forces to RAMSI influenced future adjustments. Not least of these was the establishment of the IDG, which provided a section dedicated to managing the increasing number of AFP personnel engaged in overseas contingencies. This helped to provide the resources necessary to foster such a specialisation. In 2008, then–Assistant Commissioner of the IDG, Paul Jevtovic, alluded to some of these changes. According to Jevtovic, in the early years of missions such as RAMSI, AFP deployments were more about "getting people offshore, but as the missions have evolved along with our understanding of the challenges, we now advertise specific positions."[29] During the course of the RAMSI operation, language was one skill set that slowly became valued as a significant benefit to effective engagement, especially for the police. It was not until mid-2006, however, that the PPF made lessons in Pidgin compulsory for all new members not from pidgin-speaking countries.[30] Despite some early snags, it is important to note that the AFP took care to attain a level of self-sufficiency, even though deploying had not been part of its culture for long. As one senior police official noted, "The AFP sent a 'police organisation' to RAMSI, rather than just policemen. We sent full units with HR [human resources], logistics capabilities, and other support."[31]

As the security situation greatly improved, within the first nine months of the mission, the civilian participants in RAMSI outnumbered the military contingent. By March 2004, the number of ADF in the country decreased from a peak of 1,800 down to 700 and, by the end of the year, whittled down to just more than 60 personnel.[32] Such a drastic drawdown of force protection would later prove premature.

---

[29] Australian Senate Standing Committee on Foreign Affairs, Defence and Trade, "Australia's Involvement in Peacekeeping Operations," August 2008, p. 136.

[30] O'Callaghan, 2008, p. 190.

[31] Interior with senior official, August 2015.

[32] Glenn, 2007, pp. 35–36.

Addressing and Overcoming Cultural Issues

Combining a diverse number of agencies under one operational command inevitably led to a period of adjustment, as those involved learned how best to work with their whole-of-government colleagues in a manner that placed RAMSI in the best possible position to succeed. Over the years, some of the cultural issues were addressed and overcome, while others lingered. Importantly, interviewees who had RAMSI experience unanimously felt that there was never an instance in which a cultural difference seriously impeded the progress of the operation. As a senior military official stated, "I cannot recall any issues on the ground that couldn't be talked through."[33] Nevertheless, some of the lessons of this transition should be useful for future contingencies.

Perhaps most important to the early successes of RAMSI was the fact that the security services involved had to work in close coordination to instil the level of stability necessary for other goals to be reached. Generally speaking, these were positive. As a senior civilian official argued, because RAMSI was a police-led operation, the relationship between AFP and ADF was critical, and disagreements were worked out. A senior military official recalled that the ADF worked closely with AFP and, if necessary, one was able to defer a lead role to the other, depending on the phase of the operation and the security environment.[34] Some level of adjustment was still required, however. A senior AFP official felt that, despite making headway since East Timor and Bougainville, there were still AFP-ADF cultural issues in RAMSI.

An interagency exercise prior to RAMSI was helpful in managing expectations and clearing some misunderstandings. It did not, however, resolve all issues related to the whole-of-government aspects of the mission. A senior military official argued that a big deficiency of the initial RAMSI deployment was not having an agreed-upon memorandum of understanding between the ADF and AFP that outlined the relationship prior to deploying. According to the official, the AFP operated under the impression that the ADF worked for them. More broadly, the non-military components of RAMSI had some precon-

---

[33] Interview with senior official, August 2015.

[34] Interview with senior official, August 2015.

ceived notions of what the military element would be able to do. In short, the Defence official concluded, the ADF was seen as a subordinate element.

Cultural differences were also apparent in the way the AFP and ADF determined and prepared for operations. According to a senior ADF official, the AFP kept coming up with ideas of how to implement the mission without a full understanding of what the military would need to do in terms of planning and operationalising to carry it out. For instance, the AFP wanted to open a number of outposts, but did not understand that, in some areas, roughly 50 military personnel were required for each site to provide security, medical assistance, communications, and a host of other requirements not typically planned for by the police. A senior AFP official agreed with this assessment, offering an example from a different perspective: AFP worked with ADF to get its forces to realise that one cannot plan everything exhaustively, although the AFP did learn and come to appreciate that the ADF had to go through certain processes to get things done.

Then–Lieutenant Colonel John Hutcheson, who commanded the Australian military component of the RAMSI mission from March through August 2004, voiced similar sentiment in a journal article published shortly after his return. Referring to the "proactive planning culture" of the ADF and the "largely reactive" nature of the police mission, Lieutenant Colonel Hutcheson stated that

> the police approach led to many short-notice requests for military support, an inability to prioritise tasks (and assets) to achieve a particular outcome and a tendency to take inadequate force protection measures.[35]

Once again, these differences did not demonstrably inhibit operations in the Solomon Islands. If, however, the security environment were not so permissive, such disconnects could have had dire consequences.

---

[35] John Hutcheson, "Helping a Friend: An Australian Military Commander's Perspective on the Regional Assistance Mission to the Solomon Islands," *Australian Army Journal*, Vol. 2, No. 2, Autumn 2004, p. 48.

Enabling Multifaceted Coordination: Agencies and Allies

In the context of RAMSI, coordination was a dual effort, incorporating both the Australian whole-of-government and the multinational identity of the coalition. On the ground, one former senior official noted that getting the Australian coordination right on its own was tremendously challenging, adding light-heartedly that, after doing that, discussions with the Solomon Islands' Prime Minister were easy. For the first couple of months of the operation, daily meetings were held among a senior-level Executive Group, which fostered good coordination. In time, the principals agreed there was no need to meet daily and so reduced them to three and then two times per week. Once per week there would be a videoteleconference (VTC) that included all of the relevant agency representatives in Canberra. The executive team also had a representative from New Zealand, and members of the New Zealand High Commission would also take part in VTCs from Canberra. In Canberra, there were weekly meetings between the CDF and police commissioner during RAMSI.

While there was a mechanism put in place early in the mission, there were still challenges getting the various agencies to work closely together. As a senior civilian official argued,

> Habits of coordination had to be instilled in agencies that had rarely worked together before. In RAMSI, I learned that the instincts of interagency coordination do not come naturally to everyone.[36]

Coordination was hindered by a lack of protocols in place to foster intelligence sharing. This impacted both the coalition and the Australian interagency community. A New Zealand officer involved in RAMSI identified intelligence sharing as "a real problem," noting that the Australians appeared to be concerned about maintaining their close relations regarding intelligence sharing with the United States to the detriment of their relationship with New Zealand and the rest

---

[36] Interview with former senior official, August 2015.

of the RAMSI coalition.[37] Even among Australian agencies, there was no track record of cooperating when it came to intelligence, which made for a sometimes-awkward arrangement. Once in the field, it became clear that the various agencies that deployed their own intelligence capabilities had differences in approach, the types of information they needed, and the ways in which intelligence was used to enhance respective enterprises.[38]

Progress? Reporting and Assessment During RAMSI

Reporting and assessment are important components of any intervention, particularly one with a multifaceted strategy. At the outset of RAMSI, all reporting—including that which was made available to the media and intended exclusively for senior officials in Canberra— was managed by the Special Coordinator. Being the face of RAMSI was a major aspect of Warner's time in the Solomon Islands, and he took on most media interviews and press conferences or decided who would make public pronouncements in his stead. The DFAT component of RAMSI, in line with their more-typical responsibilities, would also draft all cables to Canberra, although the Executive Committee would be permitted to view initial versions relevant to their respective responsibilities. The Daily Cable provided a comprehensive report of the day's events and became important. A weekly roundup—in time reduced to bi-weekly—was also sent out; it periodically included a statement about the future of the operation. Additionally, the ADF maintained some reporting through its own chain of command. The AFP was less formal, although its leadership was often in contact with leadership in Canberra by telephone and email.

Whether the fact that the initial phases of RAMSI were unanimously seen as a success or whether it was due to the unique whole-of-government posture of the operation, assessment did not play a significant role in the earlier years. When asked about how progress was assessed, one former senior civilian official stated it was done through regular meetings. Another senior civilian official admitted, "We relied

---

[37] Glenn, 2007, p. 102.

[38] Glenn, 2007, p. 76.

on our gut instincts for the first couple of years on how things were going."[39] It was not until 2005 that the RAMSI staff submitted a performance review and, around this same period, an interagency Performance Assessment Working Group was established for RAMSI and annual reports began being produced.

In the early days of the operation, the most comprehensive engagement for planning and assessing progress was a series of two-day planning sessions that occurred every six months. Initiated by Warner and continued by his successor, James Batley, these became known as "Super Planning Days" and incorporated senior leadership from Canberra. Interviewees involved in RAMSI during this period felt that these were productive, although little detail was provided about the degree to which this fostered a more-formalised assessment process. For their part, the PPF did not implement its first formal, robust performance assessment until March 2012.[40]

Interviewees offered some insights about why it took more than two years for a standardised assessment product to be developed. One mentioned that, politically, there was a general acceptance for these types of interventions in Australia, thus there was little to no political pressure from Canberra for detailed assessment reports. A former senior AusAID official noted that the concept of metric, while known to AusAID representatives, is foreign to DFAT, as they do not have a track record of having to manage complex programs for longer periods of time.

Election Riots and the Return of the ADF in 2006

After nearly three years of relative peace in the Solomon Islands, riots broke out shortly after the first national election of the RAMSI era was held. Prior to this happening, there is some evidence that there was a lull in the level of focus being given to RAMSI. One former senior civilian official said that it seemed that, prior to the 2006 crisis, the officials in Canberra lost attention about what was going on in the Solomon Islands. At the time, only 63 military personnel were on the

---

[39] Interview with senior official, August 2015.

[40] Hayward-Jones, 2014, p. 12.

ground, for the most part serving as added security at Honiara prison. Virtually none were available to reinforce the PPF personnel, who were becoming overwhelmed. Moreover, the head of the PPF at the time, Will Jamieson, stated publicly that there was no intelligence to suggest that the ingredients were in place for such a coordinated level of disorder.[41]

There was a creeping crisis that the PPF initially felt it could stay on top of in the run-up to the elections. Ultimately, however, it was the Royal Solomon Islands Police Commissioner (who was from the AFP) who made the determination that ADF troops would indeed be necessary. Upon this, the Special Coordinator conveyed the message to Foreign Minister Downer. During the 2006 troop increase in the Solomon Islands, the existing interagency structure on the ground was retained, and the extra troops added to that. Drawn mostly from Australia and New Zealand, the military contingent was quickly raised to 430, while 120 additional police were sent to raise the PPF's count to more than 450.[42]

Unclear and Confounding Issues

A number of issues arose during the course of the RAMSI mission that were unpredictable or otherwise posed a challenge to the RAMSI mandate. Many of these were directly tied to the fundamental question of how involved Australia and its regional allies should be in addressing some of the root political issues that contributed to the disintegration of order in the first place. Protecting the longevity of its efforts while remaining welcome in the country was a fine line RAMSI had to maintain.

Although the RAMSI mandate comprehensively outlined the participants of the mission and the rules of engagement under which they would operate, determining how, or even if, to address key issues beyond the restoration of security was left to the participants.

---

[41] O'Callaghan, 2008, p. 192.

[42] O'Callaghan, 2008, p. 191.

For instance, there was a debate in Australia regarding how involved RAMSI should be in the reconciliation process. Some Solomon Islands officials wanted Australia to play a leading role because it could be seen as neutral, but many in Australia were concerned of the optics involved with potentially being received as neocolonial. There were also tensions within Australia over how to deal with corruption. Many of the ministries being assisted were involved with stealing, and many of the political elite were culpable in expansive corruption.

These deep-seated issues were never sufficiently resolved, playing into questions about the longevity of the investments RAMSI was making, at high expense to Australia. At least one interviewee felt that the Australian Government could have been more assertive at the outset. The interviewee argued that having requested assistance from Australia and New Zealand for some time, the government of the Solomon Islands was eager to enable the intervention and might have been amenable to negotiations, which would look for more commitments from the Solomon Islands' side concerning transparency, accountability, and political reform in return for significant Australian assistance.

Instead, such fundamental changes were eschewed. Under the guidelines of the RAMSI Treaty, Australia now had to maintain the support of much of the political elite involved in the destabilisation of the country in the first place. Once security was restored, maintaining this support proved more challenging, as some members of the political elite expected to once again prosper from corruption now that the militia leaders had been neutralised. It was mentioned that individuals such as Manasseh Sogavare and other local politicians were threatened by RAMSI. With little appetite for making substantive political changes, they refocused their efforts on securing assistance from the coalition until their support for RAMSI could be withdrawn. This was problematic, however, because RAMSI maintained the widespread support of citizens of the Solomon Islands. As one former senior civilian official put it, RAMSI fell into a trap. In essence, it set itself up as an alternative to the provisions of governance and let the mainly corrupt and ineffectual political elite off the hook. Whether or not RAMSI has done anything to address the underlying sociopolitical factors that nearly led to the collapse of the state in the first place remains inconclusive.

Risk of Unforeseen Contingencies: Honiara Prison

One important issue not covered in the planning process for RAMSI was the state of the prison system in the Solomon Islands and how an expected influx of inmates might stress the system. Neither the ADF nor the AFP wanted to guard or manage a prison. This created some friction among the RAMSI contingent and subsequently in Canberra, which had never before dealt with this. The ADF initially refused to permanently devote an infantry detachment to guard the prison, arguing that they were not trained to the task. By late 2003, the issue had come to a head, and a firm decision had to be made.

As a former senior civilian official explained, the prison became a major point of contention. The question was eventually sent to Canberra for resolution by the NSC, which delegated the ADF with lead responsibility for managing the prison. According to a former senior civilian official deployed with RAMSI, the topic had become so divisive that those in country made a point not to bring it up at the interagency coordination meetings. Summarising a key lesson from such an operation, another former senior civilian official offered, "We needed more thought on what to do once the militias were arrested."[43] Had the issue been considered during the planning phase of RAMSI, it is likely that some of the discord could have been avoided. And while every contingency cannot be accounted for prior to the commencement of an operation, especially one as multifaceted as RAMSI, oversights that do not clearly fall under the auspices of a particular agency can later prove to be disruptive.

Conclusion

Although there are many lessons from RAMSI that should be incorporated into any future whole-of-government intervention, it must be stated clearly that, among those interviewed, the operation on the whole represented a great achievement of interagency coordination. As a former senior civilian official proclaimed, "RAMSI was the best

---

[43] Interview with former senior official, August 2015.

example of a whole-of-government effort I saw in 13 years at DFAT."[44] Another former senior civilian said that they have never experienced before or since that level of interagency coordination in the Australian bureaucracy. A former senior military official argued that, in general, for these types of missions to succeed, one needs a clear concept of mission and political conviction. They went on to praise the senior levels of the Australian Government for providing this, at least at the beginning. They went on, however, to state that the "timing drifted" and that, "Our mandate was clear, but many aspects were left open-ended, we were not definitive on what constituted success or the end of the mission."[45]

Relatedly, a number of interviewees questioned the clarity of the RAMSI mission and insinuated this contributed to the extension of the operation. Unlike in East Timor or even Bougainville, the RAMSI mission endeavoured to address a multitude of civic shortfalls and presented Australian policymakers with a unique challenge that was never comprehensively addressed. A former senior civilian official argued that, despite a clear mandate, a clear, comprehensive list of objectives was never established. Another former senior civilian official stated bluntly, "I'm not sure the Australian Government really knew what it was doing at the outset of RAMSI. I'm not sure there were clear, comprehensive objectives."[46] Yet another former senior civilian official wondered if enough consideration was given to ensuring that the efforts undertaken could be handed over to local officials, stating, "I am unsure Australian officials did a good job building local capacity so that Solomon officials could once again take over."[47] Writing in 2014, one former Australian official who served in the Solomon Islands argued that one of Australia's greatest failures of the RAMSI mission was "the inability to conceive and execute an exit."[48] Thus,

---

[44] Interview with former senior official, August 2015.

[45] Interview with former senior official, August 2015.

[46] Interview with former senior official, August 2015.

[47] Interview with former senior official, August 2015.

[48] Hayward-Jones, 2014, p. 8.

while whole-of-government coordination on the ground in the Solomon Islands proved generally sound, a deficiency of strategic-level synchronisation in Canberra allowed for a mission that lingered on with an ever-increasing price tag and without an agreed upon conclusion.

More consideration could also have been taken in the planning phase to acclimatise interagency partners to the capabilities and limitations of their partner agencies. While the pre-deployment exercise carried out by interagency representatives was widely viewed as valuable, it did not sufficiently define the roles and limitations of the various participants once in theatre. As a senior military official noted, the key players from all the relevant agencies should have sat down together prior to deployment to discuss such particulars: "This is what I can and can't do. This is what I can and can't provide. It would've taken 20 minutes and been very useful."[49]

As the duration of RAMSI became longer and longer, there is evidence to suggest that the enthusiasm for comprehensive coordination gave way to a more-disconnected collection of tasks. A senior civilian official felt that, in the later years of RAMSI, interactions among the various agencies became a bit stale and programmatic. People began settling in and perhaps paid less attention to what really mattered with regard to what would sustain in the longer term. Australia, they argued, collectively took its eye off of core nation-building requirements, such as reconciliation and other ways to build social cohesion. RAMSI focused too much on implementing established programs and projects, but not on working with the church and other influential civil society elements. A former senior AusAID official classified it as a classic development mistake: focusing on doing the projects without addressing the root of the issues.

Too often, these projects did not incorporate a plan for the eventual end of RAMSI and the handing off of responsibilities to Solomon Islands counterparts. Dependencies were built up, especially among some Treasury, Finance, and Health officials who were placed directly into Solomon Island ministries without a capacity-building mandate. As a senior civilian official put it, RAMSI overly focused on the core

---

[49] Interview with senior official, August 2015.

issue of stabilisation and less on how to bring Solomon Islands officials along. As early as 2005, Solomon Islanders developed a local saying, "Weitm olketa RAMSI bae kam stretm" (Wait for RAMSI to come and fix it).[50] Moreover, when RAMSI fixed or developed something, its benefits would sometimes be short lived if it was built to a standard that proved to be either too expensive or complex for the Solomon Islands to sustain.[51]

It was initially expected that RAMSI would cost roughly $85 million AUD per year for a decade, with only half of that amount being financed by Australia.[52] This would prove to be a gross underestimation. As noted, the average cost over a decade was $260 million AUD per annum, and Australia ended up paying roughly 95 percent of that.

Finally, the military planners of the RAMSI mission applied lessons from their East Timor and Bougainville experiences, though to somewhat mixed results. For instance, then–CDF Cosgrove ordered the ADF not to subdivide terrain into national domains in the Solomon Islands. Rather, everything was to be integrated. In East Timor, CDF Cosgrove assigned national contingents their own area of operations, resulting in some uncoordinated fiefdoms he did not want repeated. The decision to enforce a fully integrated military posture was also influenced by the model used in Bougainville.[53] Additionally, all officers in the initial RAMSI deployment were required to read Breen's Bougainville study. A key lesson from this was that one needed not only to confiscate and store weapons, but destroy them overtly to avoid rumours that they were being given to enemy groups. Another lesson from East Timor was not to overly interfere with the local economy, which creates high local inflation and unsustainable dependencies.

In a few cases, however, lessons from past interventions were not appropriate for RAMSI. For instance, civil-military cooperation

---

[50] Tarcisius Tara Kabutaulaka, "Australian Foreign Policy and the RAMSI Intervention in Solomon Islands," *Contemporary Pacific*, Vol. 17, No. 2, Fall 2005, p. 284.

[51] Interview with senior official, August 2015.

[52] Fraenkel, Madraiwiwi, and Okole, 2013, p. 84.

[53] Glenn, 2007, p. 98.

(CIMIC) units proved useful in reaching out and working with communities in East Timor and, as a result, were included in the initial deployment of ADF forces to RAMSI. In the Solomon Islands, however, the CIMIC personnel proved to be unfamiliar with local customs, and their presence was eventually deemed unnecessary, especially with more-experienced AusAID personnel proving more valuable for this function.

CHAPTER FIVE

Conclusions and Recommendations

In many ways, the three operations examined in this report ushered in a new era for Australia. For roughly two decades after the end of the Vietnam War, Australia was hesitant to engage in significant military operations outside its borders. Until the late-1990s, the various agencies of government did not devote much effort to preparing for the possibility that the country might have to take a leading role in interventions in the near region. Importantly, there was relatively little regular, systematic interaction between the government agencies that would soon be called upon to collaboratively serve major roles in Australian-led interventions in the South Pacific.

Although the missions in Bougainville, East Timor, and the Solomon Islands from 1998 to 2006 were relatively small operations, they all required an interagency approach in order to accomplish Australia's policy objectives. In the early years of this period, a general lack of whole-of-government processes and experience resulted in considerable improvisation; agencies not accustomed to working with each other needed to learn how to. That said, it is clear that, over the span of these operations, intragovernmental coordinating mechanisms matured considerably.

The mission, size, and duration of the three interventions examined in this report differed in important ways. Therefore, some of the insights and lessons are specific to a particular intervention. In other respects, there are important overarching insights that can be drawn from examining Bougainville, East Timor, and the Solomon Islands as a continuum. This chapter highlights and examines some of the most important issues that emerged from these operations and what the lessons might be for the future.

Overarching Whole-of-Government Insights

The NSC Provided a Structure for Whole-of-Government Coordination

It may be an example of a fortunate coincidence, but the creation of the NSC in 1996 by Prime Minister Howard's government, including its supporting processes that reached down into various cabinet ministries, was a significant step toward facilitating a whole-of-government approach to overseas interventions. (Recall that there were no immediate foreign crises looming when the NSC was formed.) Although the staffs of DFAT, AFP, the ADF, AusAID, and the intelligence agencies still lacked experience and internal processes to guide comprehensive agency-to-agency interaction at lower levels, at the highest echelon of government, the creation of the NSC established a framework that enabled a whole-of-government national security approach.

Subsequent Australian Governments have used the NSC to varying degrees. That the NSC continues to be used today at the highest level of the Australian Government is indicative of its established usefulness.[1]

Relatively Small Size of the Australian Government Allowed Important Personal Relationships to Be Built (Key to Both Interagency and Whole-of-Government Coordination)

Many interviewees stressed this point—that interactions among senior personnel within and among agencies were fundamental to enabling an interagency approach. Whether it was taking place in Canberra or on the ground in East Timor or the Solomon Islands, the ability—and willingness—to have frequent, regular, interaction at the senior and upper-middle management levels greatly aided the interagency process. In the early years (1998–2001), this was more of a challenge

---

[1]   Australian Government, "National Security Committee," undated.

because agencies were not familiar with one another and regular inter-action was something that had to be learned. Prior to the Bougainville and INTERFET deployments, it was rare for the ADF and AFP, for example, to work with each other. Even DFAT and the ADF did not have a regular, systematic, way of coordination and de-confliction. It should be noted that, however, at the executive level, the NSC process mentioned above created a framework that ensured agency-to-agency interaction.

Even within agencies, the personal relationships among senior personnel meant that lessons learned (including what worked well and where the problems were) from ongoing operations could be quickly disseminated among senior personnel. Those insights often went down to the middle and lower levels of an organisation. For example, then–Major General Cosgrove's important experiences from INTERFET were influential in reshaping ADF command and control protocols for the whole-of-government environment after he was appointed CDF. The relatively small size of the ADF contributed directly to this process.

Much changed by the time of the 2003 RAMSI operation in the Solomon Islands. During the planning for and execution of RAMSI, the leadership of the ADF, DFAT, and AFP had gained experience in interagency planning and operations. The relatively small number of senior players within the Australian national security structure meant that personal relationships could be created that contributed to inter-agency trust and the ability to work together. Experience and lessons from Bougainville and East Timor were shared and learning took place, both within agencies as well as in a whole-of-government sense.

Today, the Australian national security structure remains rela-tively small, as was the case in the 1999–2006 period. In addition to continuing to take advantage of this institutional reality, it would be beneficial in the future to increase cross-agency relationships by vari-ous means, such as including representatives from multiple agencies in training for mid- to high-level officials, sharing organisational plans, and conducting interagency exercises.

Interagency Processes Were Developed and Evolved over Time

Because of the nature of these interventions (including major international considerations, modest-to-low threat levels, and the need for holistic multiagency approaches to achieve national policy objectives), it was appropriate that DFAT be the lead agency in most cases. The one exception was the initial planning for INTERFET, where the ADF was clearly in the lead for the critical initial phase of the intervention. INTERFET preparations had to be accomplished quickly, and the intervention included the possibility that fighting could take place in East Timor or perhaps even with Indonesia. In those circumstances, it was appropriate that the military have the leading role, at least for the first few months. Even in that case, other agencies participated and were increasingly included as the intervention transitioned toward a more stable, long-term operation under UN auspices.

The NSC structure, to include its immediate subordinate entities, proved to be an appropriate mechanism to foster whole-of-government deliberation and coordination concerning overseas operations at the strategic level. Somewhat ironically, the system initiated by Prime Minister Howard in 1996 so that he "did not have to run everything" ended up permitting him to be the dominant player during times of crisis (as evidenced by his establishment of the Taylor Committee on the cusp of INTERFET).[2] Below the NSC level, the interdepartmental emergency task forces served as one of the most important structures created to foster whole-of-government cooperation. Since DFAT was normally the lead agency within government for each intervention, it was appropriate that DFAT take on the primary role of interagency coordination. Once the role of the task forces became clear throughout government, they became an accepted and useful means to facilitate whole-of-government actions both during planning and the execution phase of an operation.

The Canberra-level task forces were complemented by similar approaches that took place in the actual areas of operations. In Bougainville, the ADF commander and civilian Chief Negotiator lived adjacent to each other and shared an office. Nick Warner and James

---

Batley, the first two Special Coordinators for RAMSI were, of course, from DFAT. Although they did not have direct control of the AFP or ADF in the Solomon Islands, they were clearly responsible for coordinating the overall Australian effort in the Islands; the letter from the Prime Minister made that clear to all RAMSI participants. The daily and weekly interagency meetings that they established on the ground were instrumental in ensuring that all government agencies participating in the operation had a common understanding of any new policy guidance from Canberra. In those rare cases where a problem could not be resolved at their level in the Solomon Islands, the issue was referred to Canberra for resolution, such as the conflict between the ADF and AFP over the Rove Prison in Honiara.

Agency Cultures and Processes Were Quite Different, but Understanding Improved over Time

The internal culture of DFAT is different than that of the ADF. The police are not the same as the military. AusAID was different yet again. These differences in organisational culture and perspectives should have been expected and are probably not only unavoidable, but a good thing, since having different approaches to a problem can be useful. However, for organisations that are not familiar with one another, it can be challenging to understand how each does business and approaches a problem, and these differences are a major source of interagency friction. In the early years covered in this report, the lack of familiarity with respective processes and cultures created tension and misunderstandings. The ADF's desire for thorough, detailed, constantly evolving planning was different than the approach used by DFAT and the AFP. That DFAT did not—and often could not, due to a lack of resources and personnel—conduct detailed planning in the same manner as the ADF was a source of frustration to the military.

One of the most-important manifestations of different perspectives between the military and the other agencies was the ADF's desire that there be an identification of a time frame when troops could be withdrawn from an operation, e.g., an exit plan. This is entirely understandable from a military point of view, since the ADF's internal culture stresses preparation for combat operations. Most of the operations examined in this report covered peacekeeping and, to some extent, peace enforcement. According to one senior military official, the ADF is especially concerned about reaching a point where it becomes "just awfully comforting" to have the military present, among both other agencies and host nation officials, when there is not a specific capacity-building aspect to the operation.[3] During the research for this report, senior interviewees from the ADF, DFAT, and the police highlighted the military's persistent desire to limit its exposure in terms of both the duration and size of the force that would be committed to an operation.

The AFP had perhaps the greatest challenge since, prior to the late 1990s, the police were almost entirely focused on law enforcement within Australia. To the extent that the AFP had to consider foreign commitments prior to the late 1990s, it was generally limited to a handful of personnel deployed to locations such as Cyprus and international criminal activity such as drug smuggling. When the AFP became involved in regional interventions, its internal culture was hardly optimal for the types of operations it had to conduct, not to mention the need to now closely coordinate its actions with DFAT and the military.

Nevertheless, the police rapidly changed their focus from 1998 to the RAMSI operation of 2003. Indeed, by the time of the RAMSI deployment, it was agreed that the ADF would mostly support the police, a situation that would have been considered impossible during the INTERFET intervention of just four years earlier. By 2004, the police had created the IDG, which greatly aided its ability to plan for and manage large-scale, protracted international operations in coordination with other agencies (primarily DFAT and the military). Like the NSC, the value of this organisation is apparent from the fact that, following the integration of the IDG into the International Operations directorate in July 2015, the AFP currently manages a number of foreign deployments via a dedicated apparatus. Importantly, the IDG retains its major role of coordinating police planning with the rest of the agencies within the government.[4] Moreover, the AFP continues to evolve as, according to one official, it is rebuilding its deployable head-

---

[3] Interview with senior official, August 2015.

[4] Australian Federal Police, "International Deployment Group," undated.

quarters to better fuse with ADF reporting procedures. If there is anything for the AFP to improve on, they continued, it is involvement in
writing actual planning scenarios for some of the interagency planning
exercises in which the AFP takes part. There remains a tendency, the
official concluded, to just put "do police stuff" as a placeholder without
providing specific details about what this entails.[5]

Given the two decades of post-Vietnam "Defence of Australia"
strategic focus, the general lack of familiarity among the various agencies of government in the late 1990s and early 2000s is understandable
and perhaps unavoidable. There was little need or incentive for the AFP
and ADF, for example, to work with each other from the mid-1970s to
the late 1990s. Therefore, the culturally based interagency challenges
that were apparent in Bougainville, INTERFET, and RAMSI are
understandable.

The good news is that, as time passed, DFAT, the police, and
the military became more familiar with one another and learned what
it was like to plan and operate together. By the time of RAMSI, the
ADF was comfortable assuming a supporting role to the AFP. Although
they were still learning about each other and how to better integrate
their planning and operations, this was a much-better situation compared with the late 1990s, when there was essentially no interaction
between the police and military.

It should be noted that it is impossible to eliminate the differences
among organisations as disparate as DFAT, the ADF, and the police.
These organisations have fundamentally different missions that result
in, indeed require, different corporate cultures. Having different perspectives toward a problem is often a good thing. For example, in the
interventions covered in this report, DFAT took a long-term approach
toward planning, recognising that lasting solutions to the challenges
in places such as Bougainville and the Solomon Islands require many
years of effort. When it came to security, the police naturally took
an approach that minimised footprint and the use of force. The ADF
provided the greatest source of manpower and other capabilities, and
if the need arose, the military was ready to use force to stabilise the

---

5 Interview with senior official, August 2015.

situation. Because of their organisational culture, the soldiers naturally advocated for a clear mandate that could be held expeditiously and resisted becoming responsible for areas that they regarded as non-military missions.

There are a number of ways that different organisations that know they will have to work together can improve mutual understanding. For example, the extent to which DFAT and the AFP can participate in ADF planning would increase their understanding of how the military approaches a new mission. The Australian Government already invites some civilian agencies to send personnel to the Australian Command and Staff College. There may be other opportunities for civilian personnel to participate in relevant military training. Similarly, there may be opportunities for ADF personnel to participate in DFAT and AFP events and training.

Challenges That Could Impact Future Operations

The next section outlines issues that were observed in every intervention that resulted in tension within the whole-of-government process. These are issues that merit examination to see whether they have been corrected or still remain as potential challenges in the future.

Unrealistic Expectations About the Duration and Lasting Impact of Interventions

In each of the three cases considered in this report, there was an expectation, or perhaps a hope, that the intervention would be relatively short and that there would be a clear-cut process of disengagement. Bougainville was initiated to address a crisis and, after reaching a point of ambiguity, was concluded abruptly. In the case of INTERFET, the Australian Government expected the UN would quickly be able to assume the vast majority of the responsibility for helping post-independence East Timor. Expectations surrounding RAMSI were more mixed, with the ADF pushing for a limited and brief role, while other agencies understood from the outset that the mission would endure. In this case, however, the lack of clearly articulated objectives and infrequent comprehensive reviews resulted in a robust RAMSI mission that persisted for more than a decade at high financial cost. In no case was the expectation of a relatively short intervention coupled with a smooth transition to normalcy valid. Australia has remained deeply involved in all three areas. For example, Australia provided some $75 million AUD in overseas development aid to Timor-Leste in 2014–2015, and that amount was projected to grow to over $95 million AUD in 2015–2016.[6] This level of aid will probably continue for years into the future. In the case of the Solomon Islands, the numbers are even higher, with nearly $180 million AUD in aid projected for 2015–2016.[7]

The ADF was most concerned about limiting its commitments to these interventions in terms of both duration and personnel. In part, it was this institutional approach that resulted in military forces having to suddenly redeploy to both the Solomon Islands and Timor-Leste in 2006. In the case of the police, it required a significant change in the way operations were planned, and the deploying personnel managed in order to support what became multi-year commitments. The creation of the IDG is the most-prominent example of the internal change the AFP made to accommodate these operations.

When each of these interventions was conducted, the Australian Government was well aware that it was significantly increasing its existing commitments to areas that were weak, if not failing, states. While some agencies within the government (e.g., DFAT and particularly AusAID) appeared to recognise that the effort to assist these countries would require years, other agencies were less inclined or ready to make preparations for multi-year efforts. In that regard, it should be noted that Australia was fortunate that, in each of the three cases, there was minimal violence. Had the security situation been more dangerous in any or all of these interventions, the challenges of preparing for a multi-year mission would have been even greater.

---

[6] Australian Government, Department of Foreign Affairs and Trade, "Development Assistance in Timor-Leste," undated (b).

[7] Australian Government, Department of Foreign Affairs and Trade, "Development Assistance in Solomon Islands," undated (a).

Such miscalculations can be mitigated in the future with a more comprehensive articulation of the mission's objectives and the conditions under which a transition will take place, be it to a new phase or the overall conclusion. Even the INTERFET mission, which was the most straightforward of the three examined here, endured a muddled transition to UNTAET. For complex operations such as RAMSI, this is more challenging, but could have been helped by a more thorough analysis of the local political conditions required for the mission to succeed. Instead, over time, the various agencies involved became increasingly focused on their respective efforts, with little consideration of whether any gains were sustainable in lieu of more systematic changes among the political elite. Adopting clearer goals at the outset will also guide reporting and assessment requirements and help provide a baseline from which to judge progress. Despite RAMSI's multifaceted and ambitious remit, it was more than two years into the mission before an all-inclusive assessment was delivered. Clearly, over the course of any whole-of-government overseas intervention, numerous factors will impact what is ultimately achievable. Nevertheless, deliberating on and communicating overarching goals and objectives for such missions provide both policymakers and implementers with a common starting point that will facilitate more constructive analyses over the course of the effort.

Should Australia have to undertake similar operations in the future, it would be prudent that planners prepare for the possibility that the intervention might be protracted. Future planning and exercises should include the possibility that interventions could last longer than originally foreseen.

Intelligence, Reporting, and Information-Passing Procedures of Agencies Varied

A number of interviewees highlighted this issue, stating that, despite the steadily improving whole-of-government processes, there remained significant differences in the way agencies managed both information and intelligence. For example, several ADF interviewees pointed out that the military closely manages the dissemination of reports and information coming out of the operational area. According to the military, when DFAT reports were generated and the information passed from the field back to Canberra, the information would quickly be disseminated throughout the entire Australian Government. On a number of occasions, this different approach to information management resulted in interagency tension.

Another example cited was the AFP's desire to build on its crime-focused intelligence networks and processes on the ground in the operational areas. What the AFP was doing was similar to its creation of law-enforcement intelligence networks inside Australia. Nevertheless, the perception of DFAT and ADF personnel that the police had their own intelligence system, and might not be sharing the information they had generated, was obviously a point of concern to some in the other agencies.

In order to lessen the impact of disparate approaches to information sharing in future operations, an interagency-specific approach should be considered. While this may not be possible for all aspects of information management in a future operation, developing clear interagency practices prior to a crisis occurring could lessen the chances of misunderstandings. Additionally, incorporating instruction on how these agencies collect and use intelligence into training programs will help foster better cross-agency perspective.

While Existing Interpersonal Relationships Had Advantages, They Could Result in Vulnerabilities in the Future

The relatively small size of the military and international-affairs system in Australia had its advantages. Senior leaders could and did build relationships both within and among agencies that were based on trust. We saw this as a regularly recurring theme, heard from current and former personnel of every agency interviewed.

There are, however, potential disadvantages and vulnerabilities that can result from this way of doing business. First, key personnel eventually move to new jobs and, of course, retire. Although retirees will still be available for some time and are potentially useful sources of information and can offer lessons from past operations, they will not remain available forever. This Australian system of relying on relationships among senior personnel clearly had advantages and probably facilitated the rapid passing of lessons within and among agencies. It should be noted that, however, during the research process, it became clear that there were few official high-level records and after-action reports produced by any of the agencies that participated in Bougainville, East Timor, or the Solomon Islands operations. Some material from contemporary after-action reports (e.g., a 2004 report written by then–Lieutenant Colonel Frewen covering his RAMSI experience) was declassified for our use, but in general, there was little in the way of official records and reports to draw on. This, of course, made the interviews that were conducted even more important for the research process. When asked about the relative lack of official records of the operations, representatives from DFAT, the AFP, and the ADF all confirmed that this was a normal situation in Australian operations of this sort. Breen commented that there are fairly good small-unit after-action reports for most operations, but those were at a far lower level than the issues being examined in this report.

It is important to keep in mind, however, that the operations in Bougainville, East Timor, and the Solomon Islands occurred in quick succession and, in some instances, overlapped. Thus, many of the same officials who endured some of the hard lessons of the late 1990s were able to draw on personal experiences in later years that were largely shared with their interagency colleagues. While this undoubtedly affected interagency perspectives, it masks a continued deficiency at the institutional level to ensure that the lessons from these interventions are not left to oral transmission but codified more formally so they are available for future policymakers. The ADF, like many militaries, does have such protocols in place, yet those after-action processes that do exist are primarily at the operational and tactical levels, as opposed to the strategic and whole-of-government perspective. According to one of its officials, DFAT has "sharp, reactive reflexes" and an institutional preference for dealing with a crisis as it arises.[8] This, combined with limited resources, means that, as the urgency of a crisis ebbs, officials are moved onto their next assignment and are rarely, if ever, asked to reflect on takeaways from the experience. Likewise with the

---

[8]   Interview with senior official, August 2015.

AFP, a lack of redundancy in the agency makes prioritising a lessons learned system challenging. Nevertheless, with future interventions likely to take on similar whole-of-government postures, establishing a strategic-level effort to capture the lessons of these complex operations would be beneficial.

Another potential drawback of having a small bureaucracy is the tendency for strategic-level deliberations to be held among a handful of senior officials who keep their intentions confidential until firm decisions are made. In all three of the cases examined, lower-echelon officials were kept largely in the dark about the impending operation until a final determination was made at the senior-most levels that Australia would be making overseas commitments. While, in such situations, the pace of external developments plays a factor, it is arguable that, in the case of Bougainville, East Timor, and the Solomon Islands, the agencies that would ultimately provide the personnel who would deploy could have been kept better apprised. The TMG in Bougainville had only seven weeks to form and deploy. Prior to INTERFET, increasingly assertive statements made by Cabinet officials on television helped initiate the ADF's battalion-level preparation. And, finally, despite weeks of discussions in Canberra prior to RAMSI, senior DFAT and AFP leadership had only ten weeks' notice, while the initial ADF commander was provided with only three weeks to prepare. The pattern suggests that more could have been done during the senior-level deliberation phase to allow for a less-hasty mobilisation.

Australia realised success in each of the three operations examined in this report. The good relationships that existed among the upper-middle and senior leaders who planned and conducted these missions were instrumental in fostering this. The need for a more-systematic way of ensuring that the high-level lessons are captured—from both an intra- and interagency perspective as well as a more-efficient means of keeping lower echelons of government better apprised of senior-level deliberations on potential deployments—should not be overlooked. For example, the agencies can create a mechanism to capture important insights while they are still fresh in both individual as well as organisational memories. The organisations can develop a clear expectation, if not a requirement, that each agency involved in a future whole-of-government operation needs to prepare after-action and lessons-learned reports within a specified deadline following the end of an operation.

Significantly Different Approaches Were Used to Manage Personnel in These Interventions

There were significant differences in the length that agencies deployed personnel to these operations. In keeping with the general aversion of the military toward getting overly committed to this type of operation, deployment times for the military were normally three to six months, with the shorter end of the spectrum being the norm. Volunteers representing civilian agencies, on the other hand, tended to deploy personnel longer, in some cases, over a year. AusAID, it is worth noting, oftentimes had personnel who were not formally part of the operations but who were nevertheless active in the areas in question. For the most part, these officials were on the two- to three-year rotation, typically undertaken by officials in Australia's Foreign Service.

The discussions with the AFP and DFAT indicated that both organisations expected significant positive change to take effect over years, rather than months, in the locations that are the focus of this report. That was clearly AusAID's expectation, since that organisation had already been involved in these areas for years prior to the start of the Australian-led interventions of the late 1990s. It should be noted that, while DFAT and the AFP planned for a longer-term focus compared with the military, they were still surprised how long the deployments lasted.

The different approaches to deployment lengths meant that the experience level of the personnel from the various agencies varied considerably. On several occasions, DFAT representatives mentioned that their representatives on the ground watched a constant turnover of ADF personnel, noting that the newly arrived military members would barely learn the details of what was happening in the area before it was time for them to rotate. It was also noted by several interviewees that the different deployment lengths, depending on the agency, had an effect on the morale of personnel on the ground.

In the future, there may be advantages to taking a more-consistent approach to deployment times. This approach can be taken with the knowledge that the level of activity an agency is experiencing can have significant impact on its ability to manage personnel. For example, by the 2003 RAMSI operation, the ADF was deploying increasing numbers of personnel to both Iraq and Afghanistan. When the need arose to redeploy troops to the Solomon Islands and East Timor in 2006, the ADF still had hundreds of personnel in Afghanistan.

The difficulty some agencies had in getting personnel, particularly civilians, to volunteer for these operations was another personnel-management issue. In the future, one of the conditions for employment in some agencies could be a provision that the new hire accepts the fact that overseas deployments, under difficult conditions, may be periodically required. Or, if such a step is ultimately deemed unfeasible, effort should be made to ensure that volunteering for overseas service will be viewed as a boon to one's career.

Future Operations Would Benefit from Earlier and More-Inclusive Whole-of-Government Campaign Planning

There were varying amounts of time available to plan for the three operations that were the focus of this report. Even within a particular operation, different amounts of planning time were available to the various elements of the Australian Government (e.g., the RAMSI intervention where DFAT and the AFP had considerable amounts of planning lead time, but the operational military units were given much shorter warning of the operation). In future operations, all agencies within the Australian Government would benefit from a uniform starting point for planning and a whole-of-government approach as soon as it is determined that a multiagency operation is looming. This process should include a clear delineation of roles, responsibilities, and accountabilities among agencies.

Conclusion

This report examines three important Australian-led regional interventions from 1998 to 2006. These operations ushered in a new era for

Australia. They also required much more interaction among government agencies that previously had relatively little need for whole-of-government coordination. From a relatively difficult start in the late 1990s, much had improved in terms of interagency coordination and cooperation by 2006. The Australian Government learned much from this experience.

Given Australia's role in the region, as well as the need for a whole-of-government approach to other operations that have been conducted farther away, such as Afghanistan, there is a need to continue to improve the ability to conduct sophisticated interagency and multinational operations. The lessons from the period examined in this report should provide a good basis for continued improvements for whole-of-government operations both outside and inside Australia.

References

Appleton, C. G., "Lessons Learned Bel Isi II," internal Australian Government report provided to authors, June 2002a.

————, "Post Operational Report: Operation Bel Isi II," copy of document provided to authors, June 7, 2002b.

Australian Agency for International Development, *Annual Report 1998–1999*, Canberra, Australia, 1999.

————, *The Contribution of Australian Aid to Papua New Guinea's Development, 1975–2000*, Evaluation and Review Series No. 34, Canberra, Australia, June 2003. As of May 3, 2016:
http://dfat.gov.au/about-us/publications/corporate/annual-reports/annual-report-1998-1999/html/index.html

Australian Federal Police, "International Deployment Group," undated. As of April 22, 2016:
http://www.afp.gov.au/policing/international-deployment-group

————, *Annual Report 1998–1999*, Canberra, Australia, October 1999.

————, *Annual Report, 2003–2004*, Canberra, Australia, November 2004.

Australian Government, "National Security Committee," undated. As of April 22, 2016:
http://www.directory.gov.au/directory?ea0_lf99_120.&organizationalUnit&e3c4 54c6-f964-4da6-ab46-2f4ece27fc25

Australian Government, Department of Defence, *Defence Annual Defence Report 1998–1999*, Canberra, Australia, 1999. As of April 22, 2016:
http://www.defence.gov.au/AnnualReports/98-99

Australian Government, Department of Foreign Affairs and Trade, "Development Assistance in Solomon Islands," undated (a). As of April 22, 2016:
http://dfat.gov.au/geo/solomon-islands/development-assistance/Pages/development-assistance-in-solomon-islands.aspx

————, "Development Assistance in Timor-Leste," undated (b). As of April 22, 2016:
http://dfat.gov.au/geo/timor-leste/development-assistance/Pages/development-assistance-in-timor-leste.aspx

————, "Appendix 3," in *Annual Report, 1999–2000*, Canberra, Australia, October 3, 2000. As of April 22, 2016:
http://dfat.gov.au/about-us/publications/corporate/annual-reports/annual-report-1999-2000/5/app3.html

Australian Peacekeeper and Peacemaker Veterans Association, "Operation Lagoon," undated. As of April 22, 2016:
http://www.peacekeepers.asn.au/operations/SPPKF.htm

AustralianPolitics.com, "Howard Government 1996 Cabinet Committees," March 17, 1996. As of April 22, 2016:
http://australianpolitics.com/1996/03/17/howard-govt-cabinet-committees.html

Australian Senate Standing Committee on Foreign Affairs, Defence and Trade, "Australia's Involvement in Peacekeeping Operations," August 2008.

Barrie, Chris, "Creating an Australian-Led Multinational Coalition," in John Blaxland, ed., *East Timor Intervention: A Retrospective of INTERFET*, Melbourne, Australia: Melbourne University Press, 2015.

Barry, Derek, "Woolly Days: The Sandline Crisis 10 Years On," Woolly Days website, February 11, 2007. As of April 22, 2017:
http://nebuchadnezzarwoollyd.blogspot.com/2007/02/sandline-crisis-10-years-on.html

Brady, Cynthia, and David Timberman, "The Crisis in Timor-Leste: Causes, Consequences and Options for Conflict Management and Mitigation," Washington, D.C.: United States Agency for International Development, November 2006, p. 1.

Breen, Bob, *Struggling for Self Reliance: Four Case Studies of Australian Regional Force Projection in the Late 1980s and 1990s*, Canberra, Australia: Australian National University Press, 2008.

Central Intelligence Agency, "The World Factbook: Australia-Oceania: Solomon Islands," February 29, 2016a. As of April 22, 2016:
https://www.cia.gov/library/publications/the-world-factbook/geos/bp.html

————, "The World Factbook: Australia-Oceania: Papua New Guinea," March 1, 2016b. As of April 22, 2016:
https://www.cia.gov/library/publications/the-world-factbook/geos/pp.html

————, "The World Factbook: East and Southeast Asia: Indonesia," April 18, 2016c. As of April 22, 2016:
https://www.cia.gov/library/publications/the-world-factbook/geos/id.html

Connery, David, *Crisis Policymaking: Australia and the East Timor Crisis of 1999*, Canberra, Australia: Australian National University Press, 2010.

Cosgrove, Peter, "Commanding INTERFET," in John Blaxland, ed., *East Timor Intervention: A Retrospective of INTERFET*, Melbourne, Australia: Melbourne University Press, 2015.

Dibb, Paul, "The Self-Reliant Defence of Australia: The History of an Idea," in Ron Huisken and Meredith Thatcher, eds., *History as Policy: Framing the Debate on the Future of Australia's Defence Policy*, Canberra, Australia: Australian National University Press, 2007, pp. 11–28.

Fairbrother, Richard, and David Lewis, "Unarmed Peace Monitors and Post-Conflict Situations: Practical Lessons from the Bougainville Peace Process," *International Governance and Institutions: What Significance for International Law?* 11th annual meeting, Wellington, New Zealand: July 4–6, 2003.

Fraenkel, Jon, Joni Madraiwiwi, and Henry Okole, "The RAMSI Decade: A Review of the Regional Assistance Mission to Solomon Islands, 2003–2013," July 14, 2014.

Frewen, John, "Combined Joint Task Force 635 Post Operational Report," copy provided to the authors, January 21, 2004.

Fullilove, Michael, "The Testament of Solomons: RAMSI and International State-Building," Sydney, Australia: Lowy Institute for International Policy, March 2006.

Glenn, Russell W., *Counterinsurgency in a Test Tube: Analyzing the Success of the Regional Assistance Mission to Solomon Islands (RAMSI)*, Santa Monica, Calif.: RAND Corporation, MG-551-JFCOM, 2007. As of April 22, 2016: http://www.rand.org/pubs/monographs/MG551.html

Hayward-Jones, Jenny, "Australia's Costly Investment in Solomon Islands: The Lessons of RAMSI," Sydney, Australia: The Lowy Institute, May 2014.

Hutcheson, John, "Helping a Friend: An Australian Military Commander's Perspective on the Regional Assistance Mission to the Solomon Islands," *Australian Army Journal*, Vol. 2, No. 2, Autumn 2004, pp. 47–55.

Interviews in Canberra, Australia, August 26–28, 2015.

Kabutaulaka, Tarcisius Tara, "Australian Foreign Policy and the RAMSI Intervention in Solomon Islands," *Contemporary Pacific*, Vol. 17, No. 2, Fall 2005, pp. 283–308.

Kingsbury, Damien, "The Strategic and Political Consequence of INTERFET," in John Blaxland, ed., *East Timor Intervention: A Retrospective of INTERFET*, Melbourne, Australia: Melbourne University Press, 2015.

Knollmayer, Stefan, "A Share House Magnified," *The Journal of Pacific History*, Vol. 39, No. 2, 2004, pp. 221–230.

Maley, William, "Australia and the East Timor Crisis: Some Critical Comments," *Australian Journal of International Affairs*, Vol. 54, No. 2, 2000, pp. 151–161.

O'Callaghan, Mary-Louise, "RAMSI—The Way Ahead," in Sinclair Dinnen and Stewart Firth, eds., *Politics and State Building in the Solomon Islands*, Canberra, Australia: Australian National University Press, 2008, pp. 185–192.

Regan, Anthony, "Light Intervention: Lessons from Bougainville," Washington, D.C.: United States Institute of Peace, 2010.

Ryan, Alan, "Primary Responsibility and Primary Risks: Australian Defence Force Participation in the International Force East Timor," Duntroon, Australia: Land Warfare Studies Centre, November 2000, p. 25.

Slater, Mick, "An Interview with Brigadier Mick Slater," *Australian Army Journal*, Vol. 3, No. 2, Winter 2006, pp. 9–14.

Smith, Michael G., "INTERFET and the United Nations," in John Blaxland, ed., *East Timor Intervention: A Retrospective of INTERFET*, Melbourne, Australia: Melbourne University Press, 2015.

Spark, Natascha, and Jackie Bailey, "Disarmament in Bougainville: 'Guns in Boxes,'" *International Peacekeeping*, Vol. 12, No. 4, Winter 2005, pp. 599–608.

United Nations, "Chapter VII: Action with Respect to Threats to the Peace, Breaches of the Peace, and Acts of Aggression," undated.

United Nations, Security Council, "Resolution 1264 (1999)," September 15, 1999. As of May 3, 2016: https://documents-dds-ny.un.org/doc/UNDOC/GEN/N99/264/81/PDF/N9926481.pdf

Wainwright, Elsina, *Our Failing Neighbour: Australia and the Future of the Solomon Islands*, Barton, Australia: Australian Strategic Policy Institute, June 2003.

Whalan, Jeni, "Security and Development: Australian Experiences of Peacekeeping and Peacebuilding in Solomon Islands," report delivered at a conference, January 2012.

White, Hugh, "Four Decades of the Defence of Australia: Reflections on Australian Defence Policy over the Past 40 Years," in Ron Huisken and Meredith Thatcher, eds., *History as Policy: Framing the Debate on the Future of Australia's Defence Policy*, Canberra, Australia: Australian National University Press, 2007. As of April 22, 2016: http://press.anu.edu.au/sdsc/hap/mobile_devices/index.html